The
Learning
School

CORWIN
PRESS

The Corwin Press logo—a raven striding across an open book—represents the happy union of courage and learning. We are a professional-level publisher of books and journals for K–12 educators, and we are committed to creating and providing resources that embody these qualities. Corwin's motto is "Success for All Learners."

The Learning School

A Guide to Vision-Based Leadership

Richard C. Wallace Jr.
and David E. Engel
With James E. Mooney

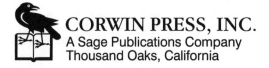
CORWIN PRESS, INC.
A Sage Publications Company
Thousand Oaks, California

For information:

Corwin Press, Inc.
A Sage Publications Company
2455 Teller Road
Thousand Oaks, California 91320
E-mail: order@corwin.sagepub.com

SAGE Publications Ltd.
6 Bonhill Street
London EC2A 4PU
United Kingdom

SAGE Publications India Pvt. Ltd.
M-32 Market
Greater Kailash I
New Delhi 110 048 India

Printed in the United States of America

Library of Congress Cataloging-in-Publication Data

Wallace, Richard C.
    The learning school: A guide to vision-based leadership / by
Richard C. Wallace, Jr., David E. Engel, with James E. Mooney.
        p. cm.
    Includes bibliographical references and index.
    ISBN 0-8039-6409-9 (pbk.: acid-free paper). — ISBN 0-8039-6408-0
(cloth: acid-free paper)
    1. Educational leadership—United States—Case studies. 2. School
management and organization—United States—Case studies.
3. Learning—Case studies. 4. Education—Aims and objectives—
United States—Case studies. I. Engel, David E. II. Mooney,
James E., Dr. III. Title.
LB2805.W3238 1997
371.2'00973—dc21   97-4831

This book is printed on acid-free paper.

97 98 99 00 01 02 03   10 9 8 7 6 5 4 3 2 1

Editorial Assistant: Kristen L. Gibson
Production Editor: Michele Lingre
Production Assistant: Karen Wiley
Copy Editor: Joyce Kuhn
Typesetter/Designer: Rebecca Evans
Cover Designer: Marcia R. Finlayson

Contents

Part II. How to Implement Vision-Based Leadership

Preface

When Martin Luther King, Jr. made his now famous "I Have a Dream" speech, he articulated a vision of a reformed social order. Today, as school reform has taken on the cast of restructuring schools, the dream of reformers can accurately be called a vision. King's dream of racial harmony has always been a possibility. The failure to achieve it does not deny its continuing relevance. Perhaps racial harmony is an "impossible ethical ideal" as Reinhold Niebuhr, one of King's academic mentors, stated (Niebuhr, 1935, p. 103). Still Niebuhr insisted that such an ideal was relevant to the human situation because it held aloft a vision of what we should morally strive to achieve.

We hold that educational leaders, first and foremost, need to develop just such a vision. Educational institutions need to be vitalized by a vision of the "better" toward which they can strive. We have heard it said that all children should learn equally well. Of course, there are differing circumstances, differing inclinations and capacities, and multiple intelligences among us all. How can we capitalize upon and use these abilities for individual development and corporate good? These are questions for educational vision.

Simply stated, we assert that vision is a prerequisite for educational leadership. Even if the vision seems impossible at the moment, it can guide us toward the better. A vision of some kind guides us all. It would be pretentious at this stage to claim that one vision is better than another. Such an evaluation only comes after one has seriously explored alternatives and thought deeply about the meaning of what one knows, what one has learned and its meaning, and what we value.

It is our conviction that educational leaders need to go through such a process of examination because a leader's vision influences and shapes practice. We also recognize that educational leadership is not for the faint-hearted. Today, there are significant struggles over the future course of the education of the public. Starting with commission reports and commentaries about the state of public education in the early 1980s, it has become apparent that any educational leader needs to be prepared to participate in reform and often restructuring. "Hot buttons" for public discourse about the future education of the public include such questions as these: To what ends should public schooling be directed? What can be done about equity for the underprivileged? What is needed to assist school graduates to be competitive in the world economy? There are even more issues that educators must examine. Educators must discover how students are genuinely involved in learning, what constitutes authentic instruction, and how one evaluates such matters. Without a vision touching on such issues, the educational leader is ill equipped.

During this century the study and practice of management have gone through several developmental phases. Theories of management were virtually unheard of before the publication in 1911 of Frederick W. Taylor's *Principles and Methods of Scientific Management.* Scientific management confidently viewed management largely in mechanistic terms. There were those, however, who saw a human factor missing. As one associated with the scientific management school stated, "We can never wholly separate the human from the mechanical side. . . . But you all see every day that the study of human relations in business and the study of operating are bound up together" (Graham, 1995, p. 27).

The *human relations approach* was one reaction to the excessively mechanistic emphasis of scientific management. Elton Mayo and others at the Harvard Graduate School of Business, impressed by the Hawthorne experiments at the Western Electric Company, saw the need for management to make the workplace a more pleasing environment. They believed that workers' productivity would be enhanced if the workers had positive feelings toward the workplace. The theory, however, was essentially paternalistic and accepted a top-down management form with little or no participation by workers in determining their working environment.

By mid-century, management theorists gave more attention to the conditions of the worker. They emphasized the personality of the manager. Successful managers, it was believed, could relate to subordinates and could elicit followers by one's persona. We will return to a critique of this theory in our analysis of Thomas Sergiovanni's work in Chapter 4.

Students of management began, by the 1960s, to focus on the culture of organizations. They posited that organizations have distinctive cultures that must first be understood in order to manage or change the culture. This, in turn, led to the emphasis in the 1970s on *situational theory* (Graham, 1995, p. 29). Situational theory saw management in holistic terms taking into account an enterprise's external and internal factors.

By the 1980s, theorists gave greater credence to general systems theory. The approach of Peter Senge (1990), author of *The Fifth Discipline*, which is analyzed in more detail in Chapter 4, represents this theory. It contains useful elements of previous theoretical management constructs. The work of Peter Senge along with Thomas Sergiovanni represents a theoretical base useful for school administrative practice in the reform climate of the end of this century and the beginning of the next.

A footnote to the above is in order. Reference has been made to situational theory. It can be attributed largely to one who was previously overlooked in the field of management theory and practice, Mary Parker Follett. Peter Drucker has called her a "prophet of management." In biblical terms, a prophet as represented in the Hebrew Bible or Old Testament was a messenger who exposed the truth about the human situation. Follett was such a figure for the study and practice of management. Her published lectures from the 1920s and '30s, at such places as the Bureau of Personnel Management in New York and at both the London School of Economics and Oxford University, provide rare insight into ideas that would later define management theory and practice. As evidence of her insight is the following:

> I have said that the leader must understand the situation, must see it as a whole, must see the inter-relation of all the parts. He must do more than this. He must see the evolving situation, the developing situation. His wisdom, his judgment, is used, not on a situation that is stationary, but on one that is changing all the

time. The ablest administrators do not merely draw logical conclusions from the array of facts of the past which their expert assistants bring to them, they have a vision of the future. (Follett, cited in Graham, 1995, p. 169)

In writing this book which highlights the importance of vision for educational leadership, the authors would enter a caveat. Much of the working life of anyone in such a leadership role is necessarily spent responding to bureaucratic demands. What may be typified as "budgets, busses, and bonds" can easily dominate a school administrator's activity. We do not wish to minimize their importance, but they can lead one to overlook a far more important objective—learning. We intend to focus on learning as the most important element in educational leadership. Frequently, we will pair the term *learning* with the modifier *authentic* after the research of Fred M. Newmann and his associates at the Center on Organization and Restructuring of Schools, University of Wisconsin-Madison. The reader may ask what constitutes authenticity in learning. There is no simple response to that question. Nevertheless, in the pages that follow we try to clarify the meaning of authenticity in learning, especially in Chapter 5. In any case, an educator's vision needs to include a promotion of learning that teaches students to think for themselves and to free themselves from strict dependence on teachers. The literature on educational theory and leadership includes a plethora of terms like *self-actualization* and *learning how to learn* that attempt to describe the authenticity in learning that we have in mind. Such notions can become little more than slogans or "rallying symbols" that often "evolve into operational doctrines in their own right," even though they "make no claim to facilitate communication or to reflect meanings" (Scheffler, 1960, pp. 36-37).

In the pages that follow we attempt to move beyond slogans by emphasizing the making of meaning as the basis for learning how to learn. In general, that is the purpose and rationale for the learning school.

Acknowledgments

The authors would like to thank Dr. James E. Mooney, Research Associate, Superintendents Academy, University of Pittsburgh, for his research and drafting of earlier versions of Chapters 4, 5, and 6. Dr. Mooney also interviewed the two superintendents of schools described in Chapter 7 and was instrumental in conceptualizing the integrated model described in Chapter 5.

The authors are also grateful to the following educators who contributed their time by providing interviews and reacting to the initial draft of Chapter 7: Mrs. Mary Ellen McBride, Principal, McCleary School, Pittsburgh, Pennsylvania; Dr. Sally Hampton, Director of Standards and Applied Learning, Fort Worth School District, Fort Worth, Texas; Dr. Richard Lalley, Superintendent of Schools, Amherst, New Hampshire; Dr. Neil Schmidt, Superintendent of Schools, Santa Monica-Malibu Unified School District, Santa Monica, California; and Dr. Betty Sue Schaughency, Superintendent, Beaver Area School District, Beaver, Pennsylvania. We are also grateful to Dr. Robert Glaser, Co-Director, Learning Research and Development Center, University of Pittsburgh, for his advice and counsel in the preparation and revision of Chapter 3.

David Engel authored Chapters 2, 4, 5, and 6. Richard C. Wallace, Jr. authored Chapters 1, 3, 7, 8, and 9. Each author provided editorial comments for chapters the other wrote.

Finally, we extend our sincere thanks to Heather Purcell Mackley, Communication Specialist for the Superintendents Academy at the University of Pittsburgh, for her editorial work and the preparation of the manuscript for publication.

About the Authors

Richard C. Wallace, Jr. is Superintendent Emeritus of the Pittsburgh, Pennsylvania, Public Schools; he is Clinical Professor of Educational Administration at the University of Pittsburgh, where he also serves as Co-Director of the Superintendents Academy. From 1980 to 1992, he led the Pittsburgh schools to a position of national and international prominence as an innovative urban school district. Programs such as the Schenley High School Teacher Center, Arts PROPEL, and Monitoring Achievement in Pittsburgh won awards or were recognized as outstanding examples of educational innovations. During his tenure, Pittsburgh was well known for its exemplary staff development programs. In 1990, he received the prestigious Harold W. McGraw, Jr. Prize in Education for restoring confidence in public education in Pittsburgh; he was the first superintendent of schools to receive this award. In 1992, the Council of the Great Cities Schools honored him with the Richard L. Green Award for contributions to urban education. In 1989, he was named Pennsylvania's Superintendent of the Year. Throughout his career, he has published over 40 articles, reports, and books. Recent publications include his 1996 book *From Vision to Practice: The Art of Educational Leadership*. He began his career as a teaching principal in rural Maine and later held positions as principal, assistant superintendent, and superintendent in Massachusetts. He also spent four years as an administrator in educational research and development institutions. He received his M.Ed. and Ed.D. from Boston College and spent a year as a postdoctoral fellow at Stanford University.

David E. Engel is H. J. Heinz Professor of Education Emeritus at the University of Pittsburgh. He was an elected member of the Board of School Directors for the Pittsburgh Pennsylvania Public Schools from 1979 to 1985 and was Board President in 1982 and 1983. During that time he was active in major reforms in the Pittsburgh Public Schools. In addition to responsibilities in the University of Pittsburgh graduate faculty, he was active in the University Senate and served as its president in 1978 and 1979. He received his doctorate from Teachers College, Columbia University and also holds degrees in theology from the Union Theological Seminary and Princeton Theological Seminary with a concentration in social ethics. He is author and editor of *Religion in Public Education* (1974) and coauthor of *Caring for Kids: A Critical Study of Urban School Leavers* (1995).

James E. Mooney has been teaching high school social studies for 29 years. He is currently employed as a civics teacher at Mount Lebanon High School near Pittsburgh, Pennsylvania. He completed his Ph.D. in foundations of education and educational administration at the University of Pittsburgh in 1990, where his academic adviser was David E. Engel. His doctoral dissertation, *Ideology in School Governance*, studied the ideological implications of school governance reform, specifically the Teacher Professionalism Program in the Pittsburgh Public Schools. He concluded that confusion about ideological implications in new governance arrangements can obstruct full realization of the goals of shared decision making. Since 1993, he has been a research associate of the Superintendents Academy, Department of Administrative and Policy Studies, School of Education, University of Pittsburgh, whose director is Richard C. Wallace, Jr. There, he has assisted in the preparation of instructional materials for doctoral students in school administration and the teaching of graduate programs in the Superintendents Academy.

PART I

Vision-Based Leadership
Beginning the Process

1

Leading With Vision

Why It Is So Important

"Where there is no vision, the people perish" (Proverbs 29:18). This proverb states an underlying thesis of this book. Leaders without vision will, at best, only manage the affairs of government, business organizations, and schools—they will not lead! Persons who carry out the work of government, business organizations, or schools who lack a vision of the future toward which they are working will, at best, participate in the effective and efficient management of the day-to-day affairs of the organization or school.

Why is vision so important? One reason is that vision energizes people to work hard to attain a better state of affairs for themselves and their institution (Nanus, 1992). The promise of a better future to which all members of an organization subscribe gives meaning to the day-to-day work. Vision builds commitment among the stakeholders to attain the desired future. A vision statement also carries within it the very words that express the organizational and individual behaviors needed to bring the vision into reality.

Leading with vision is critical to the success of schools. Educational leadership comes primarily from the person in charge of the school or district but can also come from those not officially designated as leaders. Teachers can sometimes take on significant leadership responsibility in schools to both develop and implement a vision. The superintendent of schools, the principal, or a teacher leader shoulders the responsibility to lead with vision. Effective leadership in schools can come from many sources. Superintendents and principals, as formal leaders, typically provide the parameters for the development of vision. Teachers, parents, community leaders, and in some cases, students all participate in leadership and in the development and implementation of a school's vision. We refer to those who have a vested interest in the success of a school or a district as *stakeholders.*

The burden of leadership requires that the stakeholders of the institution share in the development of the vision that will lead the organization into the future. We argue that the individual vision of the leader is a necessary but not sufficient condition to bring about a different state of affairs. A school or district's vision must be shared, ultimately, by all stakeholders. Therefore, the leader must engage stakeholders in sustained conversation to identify the values that they all share and that will form the basis for the vision statement. It is these values that form the basis of the covenant of shared values (Sergiovanni, 1992) that bonds people together in the pursuit of a better future.

In this chapter, we will explore more fully the concepts of leadership and vision and how they interact. We will provide an overview of the general content and purpose of the book. We will explore answers to the following questions: How does vision drive educational leadership? How does vision influence the organization of schools? How does vision affect learning in the schools? How does the school or district renew the vision based on experience?

Leadership and Vision

What Is Leadership?

There are many theories of leadership and thousands of research studies that have examined the concept of leadership from multiple perspectives. Leadership is one of the most studied concepts in the fields of management and political science (Yukl, 1989), and yet very little is known about how leadership really functions. Our intent here is not to review or attempt to synthesize that vast literature on leadership. Rather, we will take a pragmatic approach and discuss those salient features of leadership that we believe are most related to the topic of vision-based educational leadership.

Merriam-Webster's Collegiate Dictionary (1993) defines a *leader* as a person who has commanding authority or influence and a person who leads as a guide or conductor. *Leadership* is defined by *Webster's* as the office or position of a leader and as the capacity to lead. For the purposes of this book, we define educational leadership as the capacity to influence the future direction of the school or district. We distinguish between the formal and informal leadership of a school or district. Formal leadership includes those persons who have designated leadership titles such as superintendent, principal, lead teacher, director of instruction, and the like. Informal leadership refers to those persons who may not have formal designated titles but who influence the direction of events. Informal leaders ultimately play a significant role in the development and implementation of a school or a district's vision.

Heifetz (1994), in his book *Leadership Without Easy Answers*, writes about the problems of leadership; he cautions us that there is a difference between authority and leadership. Leadership, in Heifetz's view, is concerned with technical and adaptive problem solving. The need for technical problem solving exists when an institution is in a stable context; there is no apparent need to change the institution but a need to make it operate more effectively and efficiently. Adaptive problem solving, on the other hand, is required when an institution must respond to new threats, to changes in the environment, and to powerful forces operating in the broader social context. Leadership in a technical problem-solving situation requires one to "fix" the situation causing the problem so that the institution can continue to perform its routine operations. In adaptive situations, however, the function of leadership is to assist the institution to examine the forces influencing the need for change and engage the stakeholders in creative problem-solving activities to adapt to the operative change forces. Adaptive problem solving is very difficult and typically takes a considerable amount of time and effort.

Adaptive leadership is needed when an institution must come to grips with transformational change. The leader must first assist the stakeholders to perceive the difference between the current status of the institution and the desired future. The leader then engages the stakeholders in the following activities in order to lead the entire group to engage in productive problem solving. The leader provides structure and information to confront the issue to be solved, maintains a degree of equilibrium by managing stress, keeps the focus on the problem, and shifts the responsibility for the problem solving onto the stakeholders themselves (Heifetz, 1994, pp. 99-100).

The concept of transformational leadership is similar to adaptive leadership. Transformational leadership generally refers to efforts by leaders to create relationships based on mutual commitment and interdependence (Johnson, 1996, p. 126). The goal of transformational leadership is to share the responsibility to lead with others. When leaders gain the trust and respect of others and engage them in reciprocal leadership, they tend to eradicate the levels of the traditional leadership hierarchy. In effect, transformational leadership reduces the importance of positional leadership (e.g., principal, superintendent) and places a premium on developing participative decision-making processes. The goal of transformational leadership is to change the culture of the traditional hierarchical organization and place greater emphasis on shared responsibility and accountability (Johnson, 1996, p. 12).

For the purposes of this book, the authors subscribe to the notion that leadership must focus on engaging stakeholders in the design and implementation of the desired future of a school or district. In this respect, we subscribe to Heifetz's notion that a leader must engage stakeholders in adaptive problem solving. We also characterize our view of the leader as transformational.

We view school leaders (superintendents, principals, and teacher leaders) as engaging their peers and other stakeholders in continual discussion to clarify the school or district's vision and its implementation. We envision leaders empowering others to achieve both professional and personal fulfillment in the pursuit of their shared vision. We expect leaders to create the professional community within schools and districts to enable professionals to perform at their best for their clients. We also expect leaders to continually engage the broader community in the educational process to build and sustain the support needed to realize the vision that all stakeholders share.

What Is Vision?

Vision is a concept that refers to one's mental image of the future. Vision refers to the optimum future state of affairs that one can imagine for an individual or an institution. Vision creates the anticipated future toward which individuals and groups are willing to work. Peter Senge and his associates describe vision as "a picture of the future you seek to create, described in the present tense, as if it were happening now" (Senge, Kleiner, Roberts, Ross, & Smith, 1994, p. 302).

From another perspective, Nanus (1992) describes the concept as follows: "A vision is only an idea or an image of a more desirable future for the organization, but the right vision is an idea so energizing that it in effect jump-starts the future by calling forth the skills, talents, and resources to make it happen" (p. 8). Nanus also describes a vision as having the attributes of realism, credibility, and attractiveness. A vision is realistic when it is viewed as a natural extension of the current state of the organization; it is credible if people will be attracted to it and believe that it is achievable; it is attractive when it engages the attention and the commitment of those who will subscribe to it (Nanus, 1992).

A vision for a school or school district, for example, is expressed in a statement of a paragraph or more; it should be no longer than one page. It is ultimately a statement of the values that the stakeholders share in common about the future. It is important for a vision to be rich in imagery. A vision should call forth in the minds of stakeholders how pupils and teachers will interact in the classroom to produce the kind of learning explicit in a vision statement. It should speak to the quality of human relations and the competencies and attributes that learners will carry away from the learning environment.

A vision statement that describes the future for a school or school district provides clear direction for the activities that stakeholders will engage to bring about the desired state. A vision statement is not intended to be a one page statement of platitudes that is ultimately placed in a file or on a shelf and never used. Rather, a vision statement is a living document that is frequently reviewed to ensure that the school or district is faithful to its values. A vision statement is not a static document; it needs to be reviewed and revised based on actual experiences encountered in its implementation. Also, a vision statement needs to be revised when certain of its values have been achieved. This is because new situations may have occurred by the time that some elements have been achieved that would cause the stakeholders to generate new valued outcomes.

How Do Leadership and Vision Interact?

Vision is both an individual and a shared phenomenon. Individuals need to have thought through their own views of the future state of the school or district before they can collectively strive to reach consensus on a shared set of values that will form the basis for a school or a district's vision. This set of shared values forms the covenant to which individuals commit (Sergiovanni, 1992).

Leaders must have vision to set the course for the organization for which they are responsible. Our position is that leaders cannot possibly lead stakeholders toward the development of a common set of values to form a vision if they have no vision. Leaders need to engage others in the development of a shared vision which would necessarily include critical elements of their own personal vision. Leaders do not impose their vision upon the stakeholders, but use their own vision to guide stakeholders to consider the multifaceted elements of a belief statement to which all can commit. The end product will be a vision statement that reflects the consensus of the stakeholders. To restate our position, the leader must have vision, but cannot impose that vision on others without their participation and assent.

Obviously, if leaders cannot gain a consensus of beliefs among stakeholders that are consistent with their own values a decision has to be made. If there are no shared values then there can be no shared vision. A leader should leave a school or district when this occurs and turn the leadership over to others. Quite simply, one cannot lead effectively if there are no followers and no shared values.

Vision-based educational leadership, the major theme of this book, assumes that the leader of a school or district uses the shared values of stakeholders to create the vision statement. Once the vision statement is agreed upon, it must be widely disseminated. Individual schools should have the vision statement prominently displayed to remind everyone about the values to which the school subscribes. The vision statement also serves as a criterion to judge the actions of individuals who engage in the work of the school or district as learners, instructors, administrators, or support personnel.

Throughout this chapter, we have referred to the concept of shared vision. A shared vision means just that: It is a vision to which all stakeholders subscribe. A shared vision means that the stakeholders share a common set of values and agree as to how those values will be implemented in a school or district. The role of the leader is to ensure that sufficient discussion has taken place so that all stakeholders share common understandings and achieve consensus on those values that they share. The leader then is responsible to achieve consensus on a vision statement to which the stakeholders can agree.

The Plan for This Book

The purpose of this book is to define and describe vision-based educational leadership. We use the concept of the learning school to exemplify our purpose. Our vision of the best possible school for children, youths, professionals, and parents is one where everyone is a learner. Children and youths are engaged in the process of acquiring the knowledge and skills that they will need to continue as lifelong learners. Teachers, administrators, and support personnel need to continue learning better ways to accomplish their work. Teachers need to learn to expand their repertoire of pedagogical skills to enhance student learning. Administrators need to learn how to create the most positive and creative environment for students and teachers to continue learning. Parents need to learn how they can support teachers and their own children to pursue higher levels of learning. Community members will also need to learn about how the school is addressing the needs of its children and youth, and community members need to learn how they can participate in and support student learning.

As we proceed through this book, the reader will discover that we speak of three levels for the learning school. The first level refers to the learning of children. The second level relates to the development of a professional community where teachers, administrators, and support personnel learn how to perform their respective roles more effectively to serve the needs of students. The third level of the learning school is the community where all members join in acquiring knowledge about how they can support the learning of children and youths. In later chapters, we identify the learning school as a learning community.

To achieve this goal, we present our concepts of vision and the type of learning community that we believe is necessary to develop, implement, and continually monitor and revise the vision for the school. We review the concepts of vision, shared vision, and the process by which one arrives at a covenant of shared values to achieve a common vision. We provide examples of how schools and school districts have developed a vision for their institutions. The examples also provide descriptions of how schools or school districts moved from the concept of a vision to its implementation.

We place the concept of vision in a larger context called the *integrated model* that stresses the relationships between the vision statement, curricular and instructional practices, assessment of student learning, and the organizational structure required to achieve the vision. Our position is that there must be a reciprocal relationship among the elements of a vision if it is to have an impact on the learning of children, youths, and adults.

We then provide examples that describe how schools or school districts have developed a vision statement to guide their work and how these schools or districts translated their vision into practice. These descriptions provide examples of the stresses and strains encountered when integrating a vision into the ongoing operations of teaching, learning, and administration in schools and districts.

We also provide a brief overview of how philosophers and psychologists have described learning and knowledge and indicate how these concepts influence vision development and its ultimate operation in the schools. This review of philosophic and psychological influence is restricted to the 20th century and primarily to American writers. Our position is that leaders and followers must have well-developed understandings of the processes of learning and the influence of knowledge on the education of children and youths. One's conception of learning and knowledge directly influences the subject matter to be presented to pupils, the techniques of instruction, and the manner in which learning is affirmed. It is critically important, therefore, that there be a view of learning and knowledge that is internally consistent and that the methods used to impart knowledge and assess learning be consistent with those values. It is equally important that the organization and administration of the school reflect these same values about learning.

We view the school and the school district as a learning community. We assume that all adults (e.g., professional and support personnel and parents) in the school or district are learners along with pupils. Although the learning of adults is directed to a different level than that of pupils, the principles of learning must be viewed consistently. Adults must continually learn new skills and knowledge to develop the professional sophistication to make their vision become a reality. And they must accomplish their learning in a collaborative environment. We envision the development of a professional community where all adults participate in their own continual personal and professional development. We also believe that the environment that best stimulates personal and professional growth is one in which the concept of shared decision making thrives, particularly in relation to matters of instruction and learning. It is important that the view of how adults learn and acquire new values, knowledge, and skills be consistent with the view of how children and youths learn most effectively. It is important that the view of adults learning to govern themselves effectively also reflect these values.

Finally, we propose a set of guidelines that will enable teachers, administrators, parents, and community members to engage in the process of developing and implementing the vision. We believe that the principles we present will provide the basis for effective educational leadership to achieve the goals of the learning school and the learning community. By the time the reader finishes this book, we believe that we will have defined the terms, provided examples, and proposed principles that will enable a school or district's stakeholders to embark on the exciting and demanding journey that vision-based leadership requires. We believe that readers will be able to create, implement, and evaluate the implementation of their covenant of shared values. We believe that we will also provide the reader with an understanding of the principles that will support the type of teaching, learning, assessment, professional community, and governance structure that they envision for themselves and their clients.

How Vision Drives Educational Leadership

Translating a vision statement into the daily operations of the school is the primary work of the educational leader. Our position is that leadership can emerge from any level in an organization. In schools, teachers, parents, or administrators can take the lead for the development of a vision statement or its implementation. More often than not, however, the burden of leadership falls on those designated as leaders: superintendents, principals, and teacher leaders (department chairpersons, team leaders, instructional teacher leaders, etc.). Our vision of leadership for the learning school is consistent with the notion of adaptive leadership described by Heifetz (1994) or transformational leadership described by Johnson (1996). We believe that the primary role of the educational leader is to create the conditions that will facilitate the stakeholders to achieve a progressive evolution of their vision. Progressive evolution is achieved by making successive adaptations to the learning environment and the decision-making processes of the school or district. By using a variety of techniques, the skilled educational leader engages the major stakeholders in a thorough analysis of the current status of the school or district. Then, the effective leader engages the stakeholders in sustained conversation leading to a consensus on the steps to be taken to move the school or district to the next successive levels of performance in the pursuit of their vision.

The effective educational leader engages the stakeholders in the school or district to clarify their values regarding their views of learning, knowledge, the teaching and learning process, and how learning is to be assessed. The effective educational leader also guides the constituents in examining the ways in which the competence of learners is verified. The leader understands the limitation of standard measures of student learning and engages the stakeholders in the examination of alternative measures of learning that are consistent with their values. The effective educational leader is also skilled in gathering data on the operation of the school or district and engaging the stakeholders in an analysis of the current state of affairs. The leader then facilitates the development of action plans to reach the level of organizational functioning necessary to the achievement of the vision.

The effective educational leader at the school or district level uses the stated vision for a school or district to work with teachers, administrators, parents, and community members to accomplish the following:

- Identify the type of learning experiences (curriculum and instruction) that will be used to implement the vision
- Select or develop curricula, instructional materials, and assessment measures that are consistent with the view of learning as expressed in the vision statement
- Develop a comprehensive community engagement program to secure a broad based constituency of support for the school or district's educational program
- Develop a set of evaluative indicators that will be used to measure progress toward the stakeholders' vision and to de-

velop a means of reporting that progress to the stakeholders of the school or district.

How Vision Drives the Organization of the Schools

The organization of a school and the policies that govern it must be consistent with the vision of the school. For example, if an element of one's vision statement includes the statement that learners must become effective problem solvers, that element must be reflected in the organization and governance of the school as well. Effective problem-solving organizations typically engage stakeholders in some form of shared or consensus decision making that will determine the operations and the outcomes of the school. In the learning school, a major assumption is made that all members of the school are learners. Teachers, for example, are expected to learn how to engage in effective problem solving regarding the administration of the school and the conduct of instruction in the classroom. By developing effective and efficient procedures to analyze and solve problems, teachers, administrators, and parents become full participants in the learning community.

In the learning school, students also engage in developing effective skills of problem solving as these skills relate to academic inquiry, classroom governance issues, and schoolwide policies relating to student conduct.

Schools must organize their use of time to allow for effective problem solving. Shared or consensus decision making by stakeholders takes considerably more time than autocratic decision making. Therefore, teachers and other key stakeholders will need sufficient time built into the school schedule to allow for discussions so that all parties are fully informed regarding the issues for which decisions are required.

Schools of more than 500 students will have to develop a representative decision-making body that will deal with ongoing problem solving of the school. Teachers will need to be selected to represent their peers; the selection should reflect the organization of the school by team, department, grade level, subject matter, or other relevant variables. Similarly, parent representatives in school governance structures will have to be selected on a representational basis. Deliberations and decisions made about the school should use the vision statement as a template for decision making. Decisions made must reflect the values embedded in the vision statement.

The school's vision also affects the organizational structure at the classroom level. Our position is that teachers need to engage in the creation of a professional community among their peers for the schools to be maximally effective. If schools are organized by departments, interdisciplinary teams, or grade levels, members of those groups must engage in discussion and share decisions about students and the instructional processes. Teachers must engage in the deprivatization of practice (Louis, 1995). That is, teachers must open up their classrooms to observe each other and share practices that effectively impact on student learning. This element of the learning school requires an organizational structure that promotes the development of the professional community. Part of that organizational structure must address the time needed for teachers to observe each other, to meet and engage in extensive discussion that will lead to effective shared decision making regarding instruction, and to promote their professional learning community.

Since the learning school is built upon a covenant of shared values, the organization of the school and its mode of dealing with problem solving must reflect the values inherent in the vision. The school must become a learning community that promotes the development of learning for adults, children, and youths. All participants are viewed as learners. Children and youths engage in learning to acquire the knowledge and skills that will enable them to succeed in school and to become lifelong learners. Teachers and administrators will engage in learning to ensure that they acquire the emerging knowledge and skills of the profession so that they can most effectively serve the learning needs of children and youths. In addition, teachers, administrators, and parents in the learning community will engage in the skills of effective problem solving so that they can create a working and learning environment that maximizes the potential of all the school's stakeholders.

One of the key values of the learning school is that the organization has the capacity to continually renew itself as it strives to fulfill its vision. A vision statement itself is not a static document; it must be viewed as a dynamic statement that will be refined and revised based on the experience of the participants. This concept of organizational renewal is critical to the learning school. The school must continually assess the extent to which it is successful or unsuccessful in meeting the learning needs of its primary clients—students—and make appropriate modifications. Additionally, the school must constantly reflect upon the extent to which it is meeting the needs of the professional staff and parents. Through careful analysis of the status quo regarding the organization structure and through effective problem identification and problem solving, the learning school establishes the conditions for renewal.

The principal of the learning school plays the key role in ensuring the continual renewal of the school. It is the principal who leads all stakeholders to realize the vision of the school and constantly reminds them of their shared goals. The principal also has the responsibility to create the conditions within the organization that will promote the growth and development of the professional community. It is the principal who must facilitate the decision-making processes to ensure that the members of the learning community engage productively in its continual renewal. In effect, it is the principal who must energize the school; it takes a great deal of energy and persistence to realize the goals of the learning school. The principal must be adept at gathering data from diverse sources to monitor the progress of the school toward vision attainment. By developing indicators of quality for the learning school, the principal helps all of the stakeholders continually monitor the progress of the school toward the realization of its vision and communicate its accomplishments to the community.

How Vision Drives Learning in the School

Explicitly or implicitly, the vision statement for a school or a district typically contains statements about how children and youths will learn. Often, vision statements make direct or indirect reference to children and youths engaging in active learning experiences or in problem-solving learning. These expressed values have direct impact on the curriculum and instructional practices of the school. If, for example, the school or district expresses a value toward active learning, the majority of learning experiences will actively engage students in learning by doing as opposed to learning by listening. This is not to say that learning by listening is not valid; rather, it expresses the value that pupils should be active manipulators of their learning environment most of the time. Chapter 3 reviews the direct implications of one's values about learning as they relate to curriculum and instruction. Thus, the vision statement does have direct influence on how learning will take place in the schools.

Vision statements also tend to reflect, explicitly or implicitly, values about how the outcomes of learning will be measured. One's views of learning have significant implication for evaluation or assessment techniques that will be used to verify that student learning has actually taken place. If, for example, a value is expressed that students should construct knowledge (e.g., demonstrate that they have acquired new meaning for themselves), the manner in which the learning is assessed should reflect that value position. Students can demonstrate that they have produced new knowledge through the creation of products, projects, portfolios, exhibitions, and the like. The goal is to have the student produce something that demonstrates that they have attained understanding of a body of knowledge or a set of skills.

Using assessment measures directly related to the learning values expressed in the vision statement is critically important to the learning school. Too often, schools or school districts use standardized tests exclusively to make definitive judgments about the attainment of learning goals. In most cases, standardized tests measure very low-level skills and do not gather information commensurate with the richness of learning expressed in a vision statement. This issue is important for schools and districts who want their pupils to demonstrate that they have made meaning for themselves. A great burden is placed on teachers, principals, and parents in the learning school to create a culture to accept alternative forms of assessment which judge the effectiveness of student learning. Most schools will face the problem of weaning parents and the general public away from a total reliance on standardized test scores. The issue becomes one of being able to demonstrate that students have learned the basics measured by standardized tests but that they also can demonstrate mastery of knowledge and skills that go far beyond the limits of those tests.

The vision statement for a school or district will have significant implications for how learning is to occur in the schools and how that learning is to be verified. It is up to the teachers, principals, and parents to ensure that the school or district is faithful to the learning principles expressed in its vision statement and that the ways of measuring success in the schools reflects those values.

Vision and Continuous Renewal

Throughout this chapter, we have conveyed the notion that developing a vision is not a one-time event. A vision statement that expresses the values of the stakeholders of a school or school district is a living document. As such, it will undergo some modifications based on experience and new knowledge. Since the vision statement becomes operational only when it is translated into goals, activities, strategic plans, and action plans, it will undoubtedly take on new meaning as it is implemented.

The values that underlie the vision statement should be reviewed periodically to ensure that they are being faithfully implemented. The value statements that comprise the vision should be reviewed at least annually to ensure that they are brought up to date. Most important, teachers and administrators need to reflect on the vision statement and inquire about the fidelity of the implementation in relation to that vision. It is very important that all of the stakeholders perceive that actions taken and plans made truly reflect the values in the vision statement. This is particularly true as it relates to the quality of instruction and the quality of interpersonal relations evident in the school or district. It is also important that data gathered to affirm the implementation of the vision and the quality of student achievement reflect the values in the vision statement.

Equally important is the ability and the willingness of the stakeholders to examine operating policies and practices of the school or district to ensure that they are consistent with the vision. The development of a professional community within the school or district must also reflect the values embedded in the vision statement. The congruence between the vision statement and the work life of professionals and students must be affirmed. The school or district must ensure that the conditions exist to stimulate and support the continuing professional development of the professional staff.

As schools or districts develop annual plans, they should take the time to reflect on the vision statement and make necessary modifications. Every two to three years, the entire stakeholder group should take the time to reflect on their vision statement and test it against the reality that they experience in their daily work and learning. These activities may appear to the reader to be so obvious that they do not need repetition. However, our experience indicates that it is very easy to stray from one's vision statement in the development of policies or the implementation of administrative or instructional practices if one is not careful. Stakeholders will often reassess what they intend to do when asked this simple question: Is this policy or action consistent with our vision?

The development of a vision statement is not done for the purpose of having a written statement that can be handed out to visitors. Rather, the vision statement is something that should be conspicuously posted in a school or district and used as a yardstick to measure the behavior and actions of the stakeholders. The vision statement is not only a statement of the desired future of the school or district but the criterion to judge its daily actions and outcomes.

The principal of the school and the superintendent of the district bear the responsibility to create the conditions to promote reflection. They must provide the leadership at the school or district level to allow for time and the guidance to help the stakeholders thoughtfully reflect on their vision and its current status in the policies and practices of the school or district. Following thoughtful analysis, the principal or superintendent guides the stakeholders in making appropriate modifications to the vision statement as a means of making the vision statement a vital document that guides the continuous development of the learning school.

Summary

Vision is central to the viability of schools and other organizations. The appropriate vision for a school or district helps to build commitment among the stakeholders to achieve the values that are implicit and explicit in the vision statement. When a vision is shared among the stakeholders, it provides the basis for leaders to take action to implement it.

Leadership is critical to the implementation of vision. Vision implementation requires both adaptive leadership (Heifetz, 1994) and transformational leadership (Johnson, 1996). Adaptive leadership enables the organization to make the changes necessary to adjust to new social, economic, or educational conditions. Transformational leadership builds interdependence among the stakeholders as they share the responsibility to achieve the vision for their school or district.

Vision is a mental image of the future of a school or district (Senge, 1990). A vision should be realistic, credible, and attractive (Nanus, 1992). Vision for a school or district should be rich in imagery that provides exemplars of the behavior of stakeholders. Leaders need their own personal vision to serve as the platform to develop shared vision among stakeholders.

This book provides the reader with a brief review of philosophical thought and the contribution of psychologists to the definition of learning and knowledge. We propose the model of a learning school where everyone is a learner. Students engage in learning to acquire the knowledge, skills, and dispositions to continue as lifelong learners. Teachers and administrators learn how to serve students as learners more effectively and engage in problem solving to make the school or district a learning organization. Parents and community members learn how they can participate in supporting the school and learners who build the learning organization. We will present the concept of the professional community to indicate how teachers and administrators participate in achieving the learning school.

Educational leaders use vision to help define the learning activities for students; they use vision as the basis for curriculum development and the identification of the appropriate measures to assess student learning.

Vision also influences the organization and decision-making processes of the learning school. The vision is used as a template in decision making to ensure that actions and decisions are consistent with it.

Vision is a dynamic concept that needs to be reviewed periodically to test its adequacy. Vision will evolve as a school or district experiences its implementation. It will be modified as needed to reflect the experience of the stakeholders. In this respect, vision is critical to the continual renewal of the school or district as a learning organization.

2

Exploring Deep Beliefs About Knowledge

The First Step

We define vision, in part, as foresight of where one wants to go or what one feels needs to be achieved. It is not a fanciful notion or an activity one might ascribe to a visionary. It is not a sugar coating on one's purposes as suggested by a former president when he spoke pejoratively about the "vision thing." Nor is it synonymous with what the school administration literature calls *goals* or *objectives*. We speak of vision as an all-encompassing worldview which provides focus for what one knows, what is to be learned, and what is to be valued. In short, it is the ground on which one makes meaning.

In this chapter, we explore deep beliefs about knowledge and consider three areas: (a) challenges, or what we view positively as stepping-stones to meaning making; (b) currents in 20th-century thought, which provide bases for meaning making; and (c) the relation between knowing and learning.

Challenges for Vision of Educational Leadership

At the outset, consider three areas of thought sometimes viewed as dichotomies but that we argue are relational:

- Theory and practice
- Knowledge and learning
- The knower and the known

Each of these stepping-stones or challenges relates to the philosophical discipline of epistemology (theory of knowledge). For example, when considering the relation between theory and practice, one is involved in explaining something unproved. As such, the explanation is based on foresight or tentative knowledge (theory). Practice, presumably, will resolve the tentative character of the theory. After the fact, the theory or explanation can be confirmed or denied.

Seen in this way, a theory is potential knowledge and once confirmed by practice it is established knowledge. Such established knowledge, in turn, is used as a basis for future action (practice). A simple example will suffice. Standing in one place, as I look around 360°, the earth appears to be flat out to the horizon on all sides. Is there nothing beyond? I know better (theoretical or tentative). I have looked at maps which indicate a "beyond" past my limited vision and tentative knowledge. I have seen photographs of a globelike earth from outer space. Of course, there is more than meets the eye. The limited outpost of my eyes is extended by the established knowledge of the earth's curvature which was only a theory in the time of Galileo and Copernicus. Now I see more than I once did. As such, theory is the starting point of a continuum leading to practice. Thus, theory and practice are related.

Knowledge and learning are similarly relational. When I learn, what I learn is knowledge. Whether in a classroom or a library or in any of my day-to-day experiences, I have learning opportunities. As we shall see, knowledge is not merely the passive reception of information. It is also making meaning of the information. The philosopher John Dewey referred to such meaning making as *growth.* The knowledge one learns in one moment becomes the basis for action in subsequent experiences. Since learning leads to knowing and knowing as meaning making provides the basis for intelligent activity in subsequent moments, the process can be regarded as ongoing. What I learn becomes what I know, and that, in turn, provides me with the ground for further learning. As children develop, they learn by intermingling past with present experiences as a means of further growth.

Learning is a constant process; thus, over time one learns how to learn. Learning provides knowledge. That knowledge, whether theoretical (tentative) or practical (established), raises further questions. Those questions define what more knowledge needs to be attained. The interaction between knowledge and learning is ongoing.

If one stops the process, it is done at the expense of further learning. G. K. Chesterton once noted that there is one thought that stops thought and that is the only thought that ought to be stopped.

The one who knows is also in constant relation with the known. What is known constantly changes. In one moment it is not known whether the earth is flat or round. One may assume that it is flat, but as one proceeds on that assumption, significant questions are raised. Earth's shape is now open to question, and there is a need for more learning. Further learning answers the questions, and, in either case, something new is learned.

Stasis of knowing is never achieved because there can always be more to learn. Current knowledge is used for further action which yields new questions; that is, new learning opportunities confront us.

Vision, accordingly, is never set in a frozen form. Theory (tentative knowledge) relates to practice (post hoc actualization). In turn, the knowledge derived from current learning (combining theory with practice) becomes the basis for answering further questions. Thus, the relation between the knower and the known is ever changing. As such, vision as foresight is dynamic.

Currents of 20th-Century Thought
in Meaning Making

The theory of knowledge (epistemology) has been a central occupation of philosophy throughout the centuries. Aristotle, for example, based his epistemology on a deceptively simple question: "Ti esti?" ("What is it?" in English). What follows are leading questions such as what do we know, and how do we know it? With the great emphasis in Aristotle's thought on rhetoric, a useful axiom growing out of his philosophy can be stated as "if you can say it, then you know it," or the converse. More could be said about the enormous contribution to thinking about knowing by Aristotle and his predecessors, Plato and the pre-Socratics. Suffice it to say that their contribution was to frame the kind of issues from which one's vision may be developed.

In the 20th century, three parallel philosophic tempers have emerged that dominate the ways in which we think about knowledge. The first was articulated in the movement of *language analysis*. An extreme form of language analysis, *logical positivism*, was radically empiricistic, relying on concrete proof of all knowledge propositions based on sense experience. If a claim could not be validated by the senses, then it was not knowledge. Hence, speculative or moral notions were not regarded as knowledge. In its less radically empiricistic form, language analysis looked for clear and consistent expression of ideas. Knowing as meaning making was thus not restricted to empirical tests. Instead, John Wisdom (1957) neatly stated that "the meaning of a statement is the method of its verification" (p. 51). In other words, a statement has meaning according to its use. If I say that something is the right thing to do, I am not making an empirical claim because sense experience cannot directly validate the claim. Still, it is not "nonsense" if one can present a persuasive argument why the claim should be accepted. Of course, such normative arguments are open to dispute. Nevertheless, according to ordinary language analysis philosophy, the rightness of the claim is based on notions beyond sensory experience such as adherence to a set of moral standards. In this view, meaning making relies on ideas or notions or statements which are clear in terms of their basis.

A second philosophic temper, phenomenology, considers knowledge as situated. A fundamental distinction is made between the *natural attitude* and the *phenomenological attitude*. According to Edmund Husserl (1964), the progenitor of this movement, the contents of the mind are *phenomena* meaning, in terms of its Greek etymology, *appearances*. Typical analytic thinking supposes there is a world of objects external to the self. For the phenomenologist, however, the mind consists of appearances that are products of feeling, imagining, valuing, perceiving, thinking, remembering, prior experiences, future expectations, and so forth. It is thus the situation of the self that shapes these appearances.

Accordingly, I am not an objective observer. Instead, I am a product of my *lebenswelt* or "life world" (Kneller, 1984, p. 30). My social position, my psychological disposition, and my cultural heritage are among the significant factors that influence the way I perceive my reality. The significant problem that anyone confronts, therefore, is the problem of *intersubjectivity*. How does one subject understand another? The problem is surmounted insofar as one subject—I—engages the subjectivity of another—you—(Kneller, 1984, pp. 46-51).

Thus, phenomenology can lead to the notion that our realities are socially constructed. Peter Berger and Thomas Luckmann (1966) contend that we make our own realities. The plural voice is important.

As individuals in societies, we make things. We build huts, skyscrap-
ers, logs to forge streams, bridges, paths and roads for bikers and
horses, superhighways for cars and trucks, or skyways for airplanes.
And we make symbolic systems such as language and values. In
turn, these constructions come back to guide and control us. Our
roads determine our routes. Our buildings determine how we live
and work. Our language determines how we communicate. Our values set standards for living.

None of these life elements is a given, apart from the human
activity of construction. Does this indicate that humans are essentially free, as some existential phenomenologists (e.g., Jean-Paul Sartre)
have asserted? If human construction creates things such as physical
objects, living systems, language, and values, then human freedom
is limited within the confines of those systems. For example, even
though societal values are a human construction, individuals feel
guilt when they contravene them.

Do such phenomenological outlooks influence vision building?
At least this much: that human endeavor develops ways of living
and is enormously creative. Even children create worlds of meaning
when they make pictures or identify, through language, objects or
persons in their environment. Still, once concretized or codified,
such human constructions direct subsequent activity.

Thus, the making of meaning is a part of one's interaction with
the world as one knows it. Although one is free to make what one
will of the world, nevertheless one is limited by the where, the what,
and the how of one's world. One's vision needs to account for the
where, the what, and the how of one's life world.

The *where* of one's life world has to do with physical location and
place in society (e.g., socioeconomic status and personal and cultural
heritage). The *what* refers to significant life experiences and personal
characteristics (e.g., educational development or the impact of formative events). The *how* of one's life world relates to one's skill level
(e.g., physical skills, such as locomotion; communication skills, such
as linguistic abilities; and temperament, such as psychological outlook). Taken together, such factors influence the ways in which the
world appears to the self. Does one live in a hostile world? Of course,
that depends on temperament, skill level, and social or cultural situation. Does one have hope? Similarly, that depends on the "where,
what, and how" of one's situation.

From the phenomenological standpoint, all these matters are central to one's vision. Hence, if vision is defined primarily as foresight, then foresight will be influenced and informed by what appears to the mind.

A third current of thought or philosophic temper is found in the movement referred to as *pragmatism*, heavily influenced by the thought of such American philosophers as Charles Sumner Peirce and William James. Here, however, we restrict comment to the educational philosophy of John Dewey. Although Dewey's confidence in the scientific method emphasized a notion of experience not unlike the logical positivists, Dewey also emphasized what he called ordinary experience as the standard for meaning. Thus, practical utility rather than what stands as empirical proof is the center of a truth claim. At the same time, Dewey was not unaware of the interaction between the knower and the known (Dewey & Bentley, 1949), but he did not rely on a phenomenological method for exploring knowledge as situated. Instead, he developed a wide-ranging theory of experience (Dewey 1916, 1929, 1963).

Dewey's theory of experience as it relates to his philosophy of education can be explored in terms of three complementary dimensions: (a) environment and experience, (b) growth and experience, and (c) thinking and experience.

Environment and Experience

First, in Dewey's terms, environment is seen to be the context of experience. It is important to note that the notion of environment is not restrictive. For example, Dewey's use of the term should not be construed as limited to the home, neighborhood, or school of the child. As he puts it, environment denotes "something more than surroundings which encompass an individual" (Dewey, 1916, p. 11). The "something more" can be understood as "the specific *continuity* of the surroundings of . . . [the individual's] active tendencies" and this includes "some things which are remote in time and space from a living creature" (Dewey, 1916, p. 11). Accordingly, one's immediate setting should not be confused with one's environment as Dewey intended the term environment to connote that within one's immediate physical space there are links to a larger environment. Figuratively speaking, there are doors that lead outward to hallways that in turn lead us to other settings.

Similarly, the notion of environment is not bounded by time. The transcendence of time is perhaps best seen in places where information of other times and places can be immediately retrieved. In a library, one can experience one's heritage by reading about others who are far distant in time and space. At a computer terminal with appropriate linkage, one can experience other persons, places, and things in what has become known as *cyberspace.*

Thus, it is not just one's surroundings but many more extensive elements that serve to identify the conditions under which one thinks and works and lives. As Dewey (1916) wrote, "Environment consists of those conditions that promote or hinder, stimulate or inhibit, the *characteristic* activities of a living being" (p. 11).

The related term *experience* that Dewey uses is stated most simply as the *actual life experience of some individual.* Notice here that both environment and experience emphasize the individual at the outset. In each case, environment and experience in the early stages of human development are distinctive, yet as time progresses and the individual develops they become more and more related. One's early experience in the environment of the home becomes enlarged to include the neighborhood of the home and, through schooling, includes the larger society and culture. Therefore, as one's environment is enlarged so is one's experience and vice-versa. Accordingly, environment and experience increasingly interact, thus introducing a second variable: growth.

Growth and Experience

The interaction between experience and environment causes a person to change. The change takes place as one moves from one condition to another. Dewey refers to this change as *growth.* To use Dewey's (1916) phrase, growth is "the cumulative movement of action toward a later result" (p. 41).

The conditions requisite for growth are *dependence,* which is stipulated to mean the ability to adapt, and *plasticity,* which is stipulated to mean the ability to learn from adaptation and to modify behavior accordingly. Such learning from experience leads to the development of habits that Dewey calls *executive skills.* As one learns from experience, these executive skills or habits (not *fixed* habits, which are unacceptable in Dewey's lexicon) are the basis for successful control of one's environment. Here it should be noted that Dewey's thought seems morally neutral and does not distinguish between the development of executive skills among school administrators, social workers, and priests or bank robbers and contract killers, for example— hence the need for serious consideration of the moral basis for the development of educational vision, as we shall see in Chapter 4.

Habits are viewed by Dewey as active. They achieve something. Clearly, if habits are merely part of a thoughtless routine that does not serve to improve the conditions of life then they are detrimental. They actually put an end to what Dewey calls *plasticity*. For example, an experienced automobile driver may engage in actions that no longer demand self-conscious or deliberately thoughtful activity; nevertheless, the driver is poised to adjust to varying road conditions. If the road is icy, the driver adjusts speed and braking in order to arrive at his or her destination. Such alertness requires thought, or what we may call forethought.

The concept of growth includes both active and passive dimensions. In its active sense, growth entails a *trying*, whereas in its passive sense, growth in experience entails an *undergoing*. As Dewey (1916) explained, "When we experience something we act upon it, we do something with it; then we suffer or undergo the consequences" (p. 139). Mere activity is not an experience; activity becomes an experience when it is seen in relation to its consequences. To use Dewey's illustration, when a child sticks his or her finger into a flame, the child has not experienced anything until a connection is made between the finger in the flame and the resultant pain. Presumably, if the child did not make that connection, the consequences of the experience would not yet be learned. In other words, until consequences of an activity are learned, one does not have a complete experience. Thus, the crucial part of having an experience is thinking about it.

Thinking and Experience

The relation between thinking and experience is central to Dewey's thought. It is possible for an activity to be partial and hence without meaning. As such, when there "is no before or after . . . no retrospect nor outlook" (Dewey, 1916, p. 140), it may be accidental. Thus, learning from experience involves "a backward and forward connection between what we do to things and what we enjoy or suffer from things in consequence" (p. 140). As such, "doing becomes a trying; an experiment with the world to find out what it is like; the undergoing becomes instruction—discovery of the connection of things" (p. 140).

Therefore, learning, in Dewey's view, entails a trial and error methodology. Throughout the process, there are clear intentions, or as Dewey put it, an aim or *end in view*. The adoption or inculcation of some fact, ideology, or formula does not involve such effort as Dewey envisions. One may, for example, parrot some idea, belief, or knowledge without ever understanding its meaning. In sum, having an experience requires not mere repetition of something but a comprehension of its meaning.

In terms of vision—the focal concern of this chapter—knowing has an aim or an end in view. Once the end *is* in view, one's vision needs to anticipate that the process of further knowing will be continuous with the previously known. In Dewey's view, a vision of education has to do with "learning how to learn."

At this point, it becomes apparent that the implications for learning are manifold. We can be certain that learning requires the learning subjects to make connections between raw experience and consequences so that they can make meaning of it for future use. As a result, the learner is enabled to act with a rationale for behavior. Future experience can be investigated to find the ways to make it meaningful. That is, a process has been initiated for present and future circumstance to be incorporated in the life world of the individual.

Knowing and Learning

Knowledge and learning are interactive. In Dewey's analysis, knowledge has been treated in an active mode, especially as thinking makes connections between the active (*trying*) and passive (*undergoing*) dimensions of experience. We call this *meaning making*. It should therefore be apparent that vision for educational leadership is built around a concept of learning and the ways in which learning and knowing relate to one another.

In anyone's day-to-day experience learning is manifest. When you see someone, one of the first questions you ask yourself—even unconsciously—is "who is it?" Note its similarity to Aristotle's question (what is it?) about knowing. Here the who-is-it type question is customarily answered without much, if any, forethought. From prior experience you connect a face to a name. Learning and knowing are conjoined. That is a simple example of the kind of successful learning we use each day.

Is learning the singular process of naming some person or thing? Would that it were that simple. As pointed out by D. C. Phillips and Jonas F. Soltis (1985), "there seem to be different sorts of learning, some simple and some more complex, some involving the acquisition of knowledge and others involving the mastery of skills" (p. 5).

Classical Theory

In the view of Phillips and Soltis, there are at least six different theories of learning. They call the first *classical theory*. It consists of the contrasting positions of Plato and John Locke. For Plato, learning consists of drawing out the innate ideas of the learner. In turn, the function of teaching is to draw out and make explicit what is already innate in a learner. As such, learning is *remembering*. Plato's example, developed in his dialogue *Meno,* shows that a young slave (his illustration assumes that persons at birth are divided into social classes, with the slave class being the lowest) with proper prompting is able to recall the answer to a complex mathematical problem. In the course of the dialogue, Plato posits a soul for the slave-boy which has in a prior state known the answer to the problem. Thus, the teacher's role in the dialogue is assisting the young slave to remember what he has previously learned. As such, learning is conceived as *remembering* what is in the mind at birth, and knowledge is what is remembered.

The foundation of Plato's argument for innate ideas rests on the simile of eyesight as the parallel to knowing. That is, one learns by remembering innate ideas and knowledge as one learns the meaning of what one sees. "Now, I see it," one might say as the meaning of some experience becomes clear. Since according to Plato the meaning was innate, learning was a matter of drawing out what was already in the mind or soul. Reasoning is the process of learning, and "teaching is the process of releasing people from the chains of ignorance; but it is also clear that learning is passive, it is a matter of 'turning' and allowing the mind to see clearly" (Phillips & Soltis, 1985, p. 11). Knowledge is static and as such it is retrospective. However, this Platonic notion is unable to account for the development of new meanings. What we call research, the acquisition of new knowledge and understanding, is overlooked.

John Locke, in contrast, did not assume innate ideas. Instead, he theorized that the mind at birth was a blank tablet or slate (tabula rasa). What stimulated learning was sense experience. Such empirical stimuli imprinted the mind as we would a blank tablet. Thus, learning was a matter of decoding the stimuli encoded on the mind.

But how is it that a learner is able to understand something new? For Plato, the question was answered in terms of rendering innate ideas explicit. Locke took an alternative path. Instead of assuming that the mind contained innate ideas from birth, Locke assumed that the mind was born with innate capacities. That is, the mind at birth had dormant powers or abilities with which to make meaning.

For both sides of this classical theory, learning is construed as passive. Instruction is a matter either of making explicit what the mind already knows (innate idea) or of developing one's innate capacities. For Plato, learning is essentially remembering. For Locke, learning is tapping into innate capacities. For both, "experience is something that happens to a learner; but to more recent learning theorists, experience is something that a learner engages in, it is something that transpires as a result of the interaction between a learner and the surroundings" (Phillips & Soltis, 1985, p. 17). Consequently, this consideration moves to an analysis of behavior change as the basis of learning theory.

Behaviorism

Behavior change, or behaviorism, as the theory is typically referred to, is based on the premise that humans are *biologically continuous* with other animals (Phillips & Soltis, 1985, p. 21). An early leader in behaviorism was the American psychologist John B. Watson. He asserted, somewhat in line with the growing philosophy of logical positivism, that the study of human behavior could and should be objective. This meant that introspective reports of intentions or motivations were unreliable and unscientific. Accordingly, the focus of Watson's psychology was not the inner workings of the mind but the analysis of manifest behavior. As Watson asserted in a famous article,

> Psychology as the behaviorist views it is a purely objective experimental branch of natural science. . . . Introspection forms no essential part of its methods. . . . The behaviorist, in his efforts to

get a unitary scheme of animal response, recognizes no dividing line between man and brute. (Watson, 1913, cited in Phillips & Soltis, 1985, p. 22)

A significant precursor to Watson's position was the Russian physiologist Ivan Pavlov, who accidentally discovered that there was a consistent coincidence in his experiments with dogs in their salivation when presented with an alternative stimulus (the sounding of a bell first with food and then without the food). That is, the dog could be conditioned to salivate even when the original stimulus, food, was not present. Such classical conditioning, as Watson apparently saw it, provided a key to understanding human learning. Humans, like other animals, have built-in mechanisms to respond to specific stimuli. If a stimulus were to coincide with some human learning objective, the learning would occur, or so it was thought.

Edward L. Thorndike at Teachers College, Columbia University, a contemporary of Watson, formulated laws of learning while experimenting with the behavior of cats. Thorndike suggested that the more a link between a stimulus and some intended response is repeated, the more it will be learned (the law of exercise). Also, if the outcome of the exercise is pleasing to the senses, there is a greater likelihood it will be repeated, even internalized (the law of effect).

B. F. Skinner's further experimentation refined the notion of operant conditioning by providing the judicious application of positive reinforcement to learning situations. Skinner developed teaching machines and programmed learning booklets to take the place of a human teacher. Subsequently, computer programs have been developed to provide positive reinforcement guidance in learning programs with specified outcomes.

Note what has been assumed in the advocacy of behaviorism. Comparable to the theory of Locke, behaviorists apparently believe that there are structures, neurological or other, that facilitate understanding or connections between stimuli and responses that constitute learning. One might well question whether human action solely consists of responses to positively reinforced stimuli. What can account for the learning of abstract principles, as in Einstein's theory of relativity, or of learning something as basic as another language? Even with reinforcing techniques assisting such learning, it is not apparent why something would be learned. Thus, what constitutes knowledge for the behaviorist can be questioned.

When a student arrives at a predetermined response through a process of conditioning, what can we say the student knows? If, for example, the objective in a history lesson is to teach the fact that Columbus discovered America or in a math lesson that the sum of the angles of a triangle equals 180°, once the student learns the predetermined response, does the student "know" it to be true? In each case, there are significant counterarguments and examples, and to make meaning of these lessons, we need to take these into account. In the history example, there is a need to account for the fact that there were Native Americans before Columbus discovered the American continent, and it is possible that earlier Norse voyages predated Columbus's discovery. In the mathematical example, the proposition to be learned does not account for a triangle applied to the earth's surface, for the sum of angles would not equal 180° but 270°. If one draws a line from the North Pole to the equator, that line at the equator forms a 90° angle with the equator. Another line at the North Pole, 90° from the first when drawn to the equator meets the equator at 90°. Hence, such a triangle is not 180° but 270° in sum. As such, a behavioristic theory of learning and knowing is not sufficient to account for complex multifaceted problems.

Behaviorism has had a significant impact on current learning theory, nevertheless. In some cases, learning can be evaluated in terms of outward behavior modification. A student who has not learned what a teacher or curriculum has intended can be given reinforcement in the operant conditioning mode or be redirected in the task of learning something to arrive at an accepted conclusion. In such a case, withholding positive reinforcement (e.g., a teacher's approval or a high grade) until the intended learning task is met can be an effective means to promote some desired learning. In fact, before Skinner experimented and articulated his theory, teachers were conditioning students to behave in desired ways.

On that level, the theory of behaviorism seems to capture what is happening when learning occurs, but on another level it does not. Thomas F. Green (1971), in an extended example, shows how a student who has been conditioned to respond correctly to a historical question, such as who discovered America, could have learned very little, if anything, about the issue. In Green's example, the student received positive reinforcement each time the answer given to the question was "Columbus," which is exactly how many people learned that Columbus discovered America. But, Green wonders, what has the student learned? That Columbus discovered America? Or has the student, fundamentally, learned how to respond to the question?

At this point in the analysis, one can detect that the learning methods for knowledge acquisition promoted by behaviorism do not fully account for human learning. Another student in response to the question of who discovered America could review relevant sources and conclude that there were discoverers of America prior to Columbus. To establish that, the student would have to evaluate existing historical evidence and reason to the conclusion that Columbus's discovery was not the first (Green, 1971, pp. 30-31).

What does the learning theory of behaviorism miss? Green's illustration indicates that, beyond learning as behavioral change, learning as meaning making entails skills in problem solving that are *not* continuous with other animals. Further, if problem solving were confined to the acquisition of predetermined facts, behaviorism would seem to be sufficient to explain how learning occurs and how we acquire knowledge. However, such matters as the moral basis for knowing and knowledge use are not taken into account. Earlier, we noted that Dewey's theory of learning as growth also did not account for moral issues. Hence, morality in knowledge and learning remains an important issue and will be considered in Chapter 4.

Problem Solving and Insight

Moving along through this theoretical forest, we come to theories of learning focusing on problem solving and insight. Phillips and Soltis identify an interesting starting point in these theoretical investigations. Wolfgang Köhler, a German psychologist familiar with Thorndike's experiments with cats and the behaviorist theory of classical conditioning, expanded the problem situation in experiments in problem solving with chimpanzees.

Köhler placed a banana, the reward, outside the chimp's cage. Inside the cage were two bamboo sticks, neither of which was long enough to reach the banana but which could be put together to form a longer stick. He observed the chimpanzee try first one of the sticks and then the other to reach the banana and direct it back to the cage so that the chimp could eat it. The sticks were both too short. The

chimp sat down in the cage, apparently frustrated by failure to re-
trieve the reward, until, playing with the sticks almost idly, with one
stick in each hand, the chimp put them together, the thinner one into
the thicker, thus elongating the two. Then the chimp ran to the bars
of the cage nearest the banana and, with the newly extended stick,
successfully retrieved the reward. What seems to have occurred with
Köhler's chimpanzee is that learning may have been construed as a
process of discovery, with knowledge as the result. As Phillips and
Soltis (1985) report, "Köhler drew the conclusion that learning takes
place through an act of insight" (p. 35).

Without realizing it initially, I replicated Köhler's experiment
with my dog, Jody, who liked to play ball. On one occasion, in order
for us to play, I said, "Jody, where is your ball?" She immediately
went to the place where her leash was kept, as we usually played ball
when walking outside. The ball wasn't there. I didn't know where it
was. She looked at me. I said again, "Where is your ball?" She looked
at the leash, then looked at me. No ball. After a few moments of looking around, she moved to the living room where she lunged for the
ball under a chair and returned with it in her mouth, tail wagging.
At the time, I thought she was smiling, but that is my subjective,
unscientific inference. But hadn't Jody made a connection, had an
insight? Of course, the dog's prior experience played a role. But she
also did something that was not wholly passive or reactive.

One aspect of these experimental incidents brings to mind John
Dewey's notion of the active and passive dimensions of successful
growth in experience. For him, growth was making connections
among the things experienced. In terms of Dewey's illustration,
when a child sticks his finger into a flame and experiences pain, we
can say that he has learned if, and only if, he connects pain with the
flame. Thus, for Dewey, learning is based on active experience of the
real surroundings or the larger environment of a learner. In this
sense, learning and thinking are practical capacities through which
we come to control ourselves and our immediate environment. The
outcome or the knowledge gained from learning is the basis for making meaning.

Unlike classical theorists like Plato and Locke or behaviorists
from Watson to Skinner, Dewey and Gestalt psychologists (Gestalt
meaning organization or configuration) such as Köhler saw learning
as an active mode of problem solving. Problem solving is therefore

construed as making connections between active and passive moments of learning.

Cognitive Structures

A fourth learning theory is centered in the research of Swiss psychologist Jean Piaget. Although his reliance on a notion of gradually developing cognitive structures is no more observable than the assumptions behind prior learning theories, Piaget derived his theory from the observation of children. He posited the theory on the notion that as physical structures in humans develop so do what he calls *cognitive structures.* Such cognitive development is not without some degree of empirical warrant, for as the child develops physically, there is parallel cognitive development: intelligible words uttered and references made to familiar objects.

Consider in retrospect such development as we have experienced. During socialization in some primary association (e.g., the family) or secondary association where we are more independent (e.g., schooling at any level), we tend to ask similar questions in our quest for meaning. Whether it is the first day at preschool or elementary school or even much later in higher education, the questions are similar: What's going on here? What is expected of me? How do I best achieve what is expected? How do I relate to others?

Although the questions or developmental challenges are similar, the situation of the learner may vary in terms of years of experience, so Piaget demarcated human development in terms of stages. As such, the child initially confronts a limited environment (e.g., the hospital nursery, the crib at home, the baby carriage, or the living room floor) and interacts with it in physical terms. This *sensorimotor stage* (more or less from birth to ± age 2) entails developing *schematas*, or structures, for dealing with physical surroundings. Successful schematas like holding a spoon, drinking from a cup, crawling, walking, and so forth are internalized and repeated, constituting a simple form of what Dewey calls *executive skills.*

At the next stage, which Piaget labeled *preoperational* (± age 2-7), the child must have some concrete, physical situation to relate to because abstract conceptualization is not yet possible. In one of Piaget's experiments, children were shown two balls of clay identical in volume. One ball of clay was shaped like a sphere and the other molded into a sausagelike form. The children were asked to identify which piece of clay was larger. Typically, they chose the sausagelike form over the sphere. Thus, when confronted with the changing of a constant volume of physical objects into different forms, the child cannot see, understand, or make meaning of the concept that different forms may have the same volume.

Concrete operations (± age 7-11) is the third developmental stage. It is here that the child begins to comprehend generalized concepts and can manipulate abstractions as in simple mathematics (addition, subtraction, multiplication, and division), although it is halting and requires the buildup of experiences in trial and error. In the fourth stage (± ages 11-15), the learner begins to be able to solve abstract problems (e.g., typical test problems in mathematics or other subject areas requiring drawing conclusions from the given premises).

According to Piaget's research there are principles of development that stand out at each stage such as assimilation, accommodation, and equilibrium. An experience is assimilated at an early developmental stage, but new, more complex information from subsequent experience is not. Thus, what Piaget calls equilibrium is upset and a new schemata is required to deal with the problem. At a later developmental stage, the problem is accommodated and equilibrium restored. A nascent conceptualization takes over and is assimilated in cognitive development.

As the process from disequilibrium to equilibrium is repeated, increasingly sophisticated cognitive structures or schemata emerge. It is important to realize, however, that Piaget's theory is just that—a theory. Piaget carefully observed child behavior and reasoned that something like the stage development of his theory was occurring with the child, but there was nothing concrete within the child that he could see and empirically verify. Still, the theory provides us with an insight that allows us to have a sense of human development that we otherwise would not have. As such, Piaget's theory provides us with an explanation of dimensions of learning that may contribute to the educator's vision.

One limitation in Piaget's theory is that by employing a biological model (i.e., cognitive development parallels biological development) it is not clear, as Phillips and Soltis (1985) note, "how the account could apply to the form of learning that is of most concern to teachers, namely, the gradual mastering by a young learner of disciplines like science, mathematics, and history" (p. 51).

Advanced Organizers

A fifth approach to learning theory attempts to fill that gap. Psychologist David Ausubel developed the notion of *advanced organizers* that can facilitate learning. In effect, Ausubel presented a pedagogical tool that functions to develop the schemata Piaget has seen as the instruction that reinforces learning. As Ausubel wrote,

> These organizers are normally introduced in advance of the learning itself and are used to facilitate establishing a meaningful learning set. Advanced organizers help the learner to recognize that elements of new learning materials can be meaningfully learned by relating them to specifically relevant aspects of existing cognitive structures. (Ausubel, Novak, & Hanesian, 1978, cited in Phillips & Soltis, 1985, p. 52)

According to this theoretical viewpoint, a student can be given a structure for relating various elements of thought. To illustrate, the reader will be aware that the earlier analysis of John Dewey's philosophy was presented in such structured form. His idea of experience is best understood in relation to his concepts of environment, growth, and thinking. That can be construed as an advanced organizer intended to show interrelationships in Dewey's educational thought. In those terms, his idea of experience is central and, at the same time, related to an expansive notion of environment that entails growth and reflexive thinking to tie things together. Therefore, like Dewey, Ausubel sees making mental connections as a key to learning.

Other figures have contributed ideas to the school of thought on disciplinary structures in learning. In his book *The Process of Education,* Jerome Bruner (1960) asserted that learning depends on grasping the structure of a discipline like one or more of the sciences. "To learn structure," he stated, "is to learn how things are related" (p. 7). Joseph Schwab pushed the idea of structure of a discipline still further, suggesting that "the structure of a discipline could be analyzed in two parts: the substantive structure and the syntactical structure" (cited in Phillips & Soltis, 1985, p. 57). Substantive structure enables the learner to know what data to seek to answer a question about a given subject matter or discipline. The syntactical structure pertains, as Schwab put it, to "what its canons of evidence are and how well they can be applied" (cited in Phillips & Soltis, 1985, p. 57). Paul

Hirst amplified Schwab's theory and concluded that there were additional forms or structures of knowledge in the academic disciplines. They involve central or key concepts which form networks of relationships and are expressed in statements which can be tested by experience (note the similarity to Dewey's epistemology) and lead to skills for further exploration (cited in Phillips & Soltis, 1985, p. 57). Earlier, Philip H. Phenix (1964) in his *Realms of Meaning,* inspired in part by Jerome Bruner's work, analyzed knowledge in terms of six major types: symbolics, empirics, aesthetics, synnoetics (or personal knowledge), ethics, and synoptics. Whether there are two, six, or more structures of knowledge or realms of meaning is not the concern here. What is central is that these structural possibilities provide a background for the educational leader's vision about learning.

Information Processing or Cognitive Science

A sixth and final learning theory has been developing in recent years and, as an applied science of learning and instruction, is referred to as *cognitive science.* This approach and its implications are analyzed in Chapter 3. Here we provide a general overview of the theory and some of the questions about learning that it raises.

We begin with an analogy between the human mind and the computer. But we would also enter a word of caution at the outset: Computers and our minds may have certain gross similarities, but cognitive science does not claim that they are identical. We do know from experience that humans possess a memory, and we know that computers also have memory. They can save information in memory or some other storage unit (e.g., RAM or a floppy disk, respectively). Further, both computers and humans seem to have mechanisms for indexing what is stored. The earlier example of what occurs when you meet someone is illuminated by the computer analogy. It can describe what happens when one recognizes another person in an instant. The information that one has stored is readily retrieved and the identification quickly made. It can also help us understand the cases in which we sense we know the other person but cannot immediately recall their name. The face is familiar but not the name, so a more ponderous process of searching through our memory occurs. We ask ourselves questions to help us locate relevant data: Where did we meet? Under what circumstances? Who else was there? In time, we come up with the correct identification.

Cognitive science, however, goes beyond such a crude analogy. At the center of this theory is the notion that "the human mind works by applying elementary processes to symbol structures that represent the content of thought" (Bruer, 1993, p. 22). Symbol structures such as language and mathematics constitute links between one's external environment and the working of the mind. We observe an object or person outside of ourselves. Depending on what we observe, we assign it a symbolic label. It could be a mobile transportation vehicle, so we call it a truck or a bus or an automobile. Perhaps it flies. Is it a bird or an aircraft or Superman? We know it could only be Superman in fantasy, so it is probably a bird or an aircraft. The point is that we use symbols in language and thought to encode the meaning we make of the reality we confront. When we meet another person, we identify them or not. In either case, however, we know them or come to know them by a symbolic representation—their name. Either the name is a matter of recall from some past experience remembered or stored, or it is a new symbolic representation once we have been introduced.

We also use mathematics for symbolic representations. In the supermarket I may buy one dozen or 12 eggs and a quart of milk. The number 12 is a symbolic representation of a quantity in a base 10 system of addition. Ten is the base with 2 eggs left over, so the number, the symbolic representation, is 12. That assumes, of course, that we have agreed on a base 10 numbering system of symbolic representation. Similarly, for the quart of milk we know that the symbol, quart, consists of 2 pints or 4 half pints. But what is a pint? It is a symbol, like the quart, for a certain volume. If you lived in a society that used a different symbol system, such as the metric system, you would have to convert measures of volume to the new system. The volume of the liquid would not change. The symbolic representation of volume would change.

How we use such symbolic systems to make meaning and to guide action is what interests cognitive science. In this regard, it should be noted that although some mental operations are similar to the operations of a computer the two have distinct differences. Of course, human minds and computers have different physical properties. More significantly, a computer and a human's mind have what a computer scientist would call differing *computational architecture* (Bruer, 1993, p. 24).

We are receptors of stimuli from outside or beyond ourselves. In turn, we do something with that experience. It seems that something in the very being of our minds enables us to use sensory data or, as we might say in colloquial terms, "we make sense of it." In gross terms, that is the essence of meaning making. For meaning making to occur, it would seem that the human has some built-in capacity to make sense out of experience. That is not to suggest that we are wholly independent self-starters. Indeed, the human requires a significantly long time to mature and is dependent on others for mental as well as physical nourishment during that process. This growing up is education in its broadest sense, including nonformal as well as formal aspects.

Over time, we come to rely on inner capacities as well. Does this affirm Plato's notion of innate ideas, where education is viewed as remembering what is already innate in us? Or does it agree with Locke's view that we have innate capacities to decode the stimuli impressed on the blank tablet of the mind? We can appreciate the ingenious reasoning that led Plato and Locke to their conclusions without agreeing with them. In any case, cognitive science has probed more deeply into these matters.

In his close studies of language, Noam Chomsky (cited in Bruer, 1993) has theorized that behavioral conditioning cannot account for the human's capacity to develop and understand sentence upon sentence, many of which are original and may never have been heard or seen before. His theory of transformational grammar suggests that we process *deep structures,* sets of simple sentences, which enable us to generate spoken or written sentences or what he calls *surface structures* to communicate. Of course, no one, including Chomsky, has ever seen or heard these deep structures. But they serve to explain how we operate the symbol systems of language.

In this connection, it should be remembered that Piaget had early posited a notion of structured stages through which children pass on the way to maturity. Although some subsequent research has countered his interpretations of child and adolescent development, Piaget's theories continue to have heuristic value. Indeed, cognitive science has significantly built on his theories.

As cognitive science has progressed in research and development, it has modified and refined some of Piaget's work. More recent research dealing, for example, with the movement in learning from novice to expert has built on Piaget's earlier concepts of disequilibrium and equilibrium. As reported by Bruer (1993), "Students learn by modifying long-term memory structures. . . . They modify their structures when they encounter problems their current rules can't solve. Some children modify their structures spontaneously. . . . Other children can't" (p. 47). The significance of this finding (for our purposes of explicating what is involved in meaning making) is that this cognitive research reveals how different students learn. Assessment of the learning is useful not merely for the purpose of summative evaluation but also as an instrument to diagnose what some children need in order to learn more effectively. In turn, the research can suggest how instruction should proceed. As Robert Glaser noted, "learning assessments will not provide merely a score, a label, a grade level, or a percentile, but also *instructional scoring* that makes apparent to the student and to the teacher the requirements of increased competence" (cited in Bruer, 1993, p. 272).

Summary

What do we make of all this? What meaning is to be derived from this review of issues for educational vision, theories of knowledge, and the relation between knowledge and learning? To use meaning making as the ground for vision in educational leadership involves serious thought that challenges one's own view of knowing and learning. At the same time, it needs to account for dominant positions in the development of a theory of knowledge (epistemology) and how knowledge relates to learning.

In reviewing the various theories of knowledge and learning cited in this chapter, it is apparent that none is sufficient in and of itself. From classical learning theory, especially from John Locke, learning and knowing are based on empirical experience. In this regard, a theory of knowledge grounded in sense experience provides one way of knowing such things as the contents and processes of the natural world, but it does not provide insight into issues associated with morality.

Language analysis or the philosophy of ordinary language use provides a basis and a method for determining the clarity of linguistic expression and locution. This philosophy asks if what we say is clear, logical, and with some apparent basis. Insofar as one's vision for education needs to be communicable, such questions represent important criteria.

From the phenomenological insistence on understanding the situation of knowledge, both sociological and psychological, we appropriate ways to make meaning for our life situation and outlook (*lebenswelt*).

In pragmatism, as articulated by John Dewey, knowledge is grounded in our experience of our environment both immediate and distant. This idea of knowledge leads to meaning making, or what Dewey referred to as an end in view, which for our purposes is vision.

The appropriation of knowledge is derived from the various learning theories we have analyzed. If one subscribes to a classical theory, knowledge and learning stem from one's empirical experience (i.e., what is imprinted on the mind through the senses), but according to this view, the knowledge one gains is passive.

The behaviorist theory, similarly passive, suggests that learning occurs in response to appropriate stimuli. A learner can be conditioned to previously calculated stimuli, but has the learner learned anything new? Has the learner learned more? Learning how to learn, as a basis for making meaning, is not significantly furthered by this theory. Questions raised in this connection focus on whether what is learned is knowledge of how to answer questions with predetermined answers or knowledge about the truth of the answers.

Theories based on developmental psychology display learning modes appropriate for each level of physical and psychological development. Based on a biological model, such theories deal with cognitive capacity for ever greater mental comprehension. Without question, such understanding of human development is crucial for a vision of education.

Is there more to a vision of education? Ausubel's notion of advanced organizers suggests that learning and the development of knowledge is in some degree dependent on the way that previous knowledge is organized and represented to novice learners. The new learner does not need to discover fire and invent the wheel. What is already known in the academic disciplines does not need to be investigated again. It can be communicated in some correct form, as Bruner (1960) has suggested, and then become the basis for further investigation and learning. In short, the structure of academic disciplines is the requisite for understanding the minutiae of any field of knowledge.

The contribution of cognitive science to a vision of education pushes us to the frontier of today's educational research. Here we can find insight in how the mind works and what can enhance cognitive development.

All of this is grist for the mill of educational vision. We emphasize here, in conclusion, that there is no one best conclusion. Instead, the reader is invited to engage in a self-dialogue and dialogue with others to find meaning among the alternatives analyzed here and come to a conclusion about what makes sense for the individual reader.

A final footnote is in order, though. It will be apparent that we are not without a position in regard to these matters. What is of paramount importance is that a learning school should focus on meaning making. That entails active learning for all students as well as the development of a learning community among professionals. The next chapter deals with deep beliefs about learning and instruction. It is no secret that we believe a constructivist view is most compatible with our vision of a learning school.

3

Exploring Deep Beliefs About Learning and Teaching

The Second Step

Learning is the central purpose of schooling. In developing your personal and shared vision of education, you must think seriously about how children and youths learn most effectively. As an educational leader, you will need to think about how students learn, about the conditions that promote learning, and about how we assess learning. You should review the latest theory and research about learning. You will need to engage your fellow stakeholders in serious discussion and reflection about learning to articulate your individual and collective beliefs. The process just described will provide the foundation for you to make some important decisions about how the school or district will pursue its goals of improving student learning. To help you with this process, here we review some of the most significant developments in learning theory and research during the past 50 years.

In Chapter 2 you were introduced to six theories of learning that have had an important influence on how students acquire knowledge and skills. In this chapter, we review in more detail how these views of learning influence the selection of pedagogical techniques and demonstrate how research, theories of learning, and the practice of instruction dynamically interact. We next review the direct influence of cognitive science on our views of how classrooms might be organized for teaching and learning and then provide examples of how instructional techniques and the materials of instruction directly reflect one's views of learning.

A vision of education ultimately has to be concerned with what knowledge is of most value to students and how that knowledge is acquired. How you define learning and knowledge will determine your orientation to curriculum and instruction. The organization of the curriculum and the learning experiences of the school will determine the structure of the school and the distribution of time for instruction. Your conception of learning will determine how student knowledge and skills are ascertained. Thus, your view of learning and how it takes place is one of the chief determinants of your vision of the educational process.

Consider two simple examples. Suppose that your vision of learning is one that advocates the traditional concept of verbal reception learning as the predominant mode. That is, you believe that pupils learn best by listening to teachers and their elders and by performing learning tasks that the teachers design. You also accept the notion that the way to evaluate student learning is to have students restate exactly what teachers have said to them either orally or in writing.

An approach to education that assumes that verbal reception learning is the most effective way for students to learn will have very specific characteristics. Students will be expected to be active listeners but primarily passive learners; they will be expected to listen carefully to teachers, assimilate what they say, and do exactly what they are told. Teachers will give students advanced organizers (Ausubel, 1963) so that students will understand what teachers are saying and organize the information into the outcomes predetermined by the teacher. Tests will require students to repeat exactly what the teacher has presented. Classrooms dominated by verbal reception learning will generally be very quiet, orderly places so that children can hear clearly what the teachers are saying. Schools will be organized to promote a quiet orderliness that is consistent with verbal reception learning. Class schedules will follow a specific time schedule with no deviations. Verbal reception learning is often characterized as *classical education.*

On the other hand, let us suppose that your vision of learning is characterized by authentic pedagogy (Newmann, 1991). You believe that students should be actively engaged in making meaning from experiences that they encounter in the learning environment. You believe that the most effective way for students to learn is for them to engage in active problem finding and problem solving, and you believe that it is important for students to construct their own meaning. You believe that learning should be authentic in that it requires students to produce new knowledge for themselves rather than to only reproduce information presented by others. In other words, you expect students to actively engage in creating products and insights that reflect their own understanding of what they have studied. Because learning is to be authentic, the way in which student work is to be evaluated emphasizes uniqueness for each student. To be sure, there are criteria that are common to the evaluation of student work: It must involve disciplined inquiry, must result from extended conversations with teachers and other students, and must build upon an existing knowledge base (Newmann & Wehlage, 1993).

Schools that embrace such an approach to learning will be very active places. Students will perform much of their work in groups with either their peers or outside experts. Classrooms will be busy places characterized by movement and by extended and lively discussions with teachers and other students. Teachers will spend a great deal of their time posing questions and problems for students, and they will act as guides to student learning. The length of class periods will vary depending on the learning task at hand. The school will be organized on a flexible schedule that reflects, on a daily basis, the time needed to optimize student learning.

These brief descriptions of two different approaches to classroom instruction and learning clearly oversimplify the importance of the role of learning in building a vision of education for the common good. Yet these descriptions reflect two very different views of learning and thus imply very different instructional methods and organizational structures to support that learning. Schools embracing these two views of learning would look and sound very different from one another. Of course, the world of learning and schooling is not as easily dichotomized as it is presented above. For the most part, students engaged in active learning will need to engage in verbal reception learning in order to build the storehouse of knowledge (the conceptual framework) from which they can launch their search for personal meaning. Students, in most schools, will engage in some type of problem solving to gain new insights about some important field of knowledge. The point to be made is that how one views learning will have an important influence on one's vision of education, which in turn will influence thinking about how schools are to be organized, how instruction is delivered, what students are expected to learn, and how that learning will be measured.

This chapter has three major foci. The first is on a significant decade in American educational history, the 1960s. Specifically, we review the educational reform movement of the 1960s characterized by what is known as *Process Oriented Education*. This movement, more than any other, was significantly influenced by an approach to learning espoused by the leading cognitive psychologists and curriculum specialists of the day. The second focus is on advances in learning theory and research since the 1960s as they are reflected in research that examines how learners develop from novices to experts in a specific academic discipline. We review the work of cognitive scientists and explore the implications for schooling based on the knowledge accumulated up to the 1990s. The third focus is on a constructivist approach to learning, which finds its origins in the work of Jean Piaget and currently is enjoying a renaissance as curriculum specialists promote the concepts of teaching and learning for understanding.

Learning Theory and Curriculum in the 1960s

The curriculum reform in American schools of the 1960s was spawned by the nation's reaction to the Russian launching of *Sputnik*. The Russians had beaten the Americans into space, and this event shocked our national government into launching a number of educational initiatives to catch up to the Russians. Massive efforts were quickly started to improve the quality of math and science teaching at all levels in American schools. One of the most significant events was the passage of the Elementary and Secondary Education Act of 1965. This bold legislation provided the springboard for the federal government to intervene to improve our country's quality of education. For the first time in our history, the federal government infused millions of dollars to improve education for the nation's children.

One of the most eloquent spokespersons for the new approach to education was a cognitive psychologist, Jerome Bruner. Bruner's (1960) influential book *The Process of Education* established the framework that was to influence an approach to instruction called Process Oriented Education. This approach to curriculum was enunciated by Bruner as follows:

We begin with the hypothesis that any subject can be taught in some intellectually honest form to any child at any stage of development. It is a bold hypothesis and an essential one in thinking about the nature of curriculum. No evidence exists to contradict it; considerable evidence is being amassed that supports it. (p. 33)

Bruner's hypothesis needs to be understood in the context of a comprehensive approach to student learning that encompasses such notions as the structure of disciplines, the modes of inquiry within specific disciplines, and the notion of a spiral curriculum. The structure of disciplines refers to the concepts and generalizations that form the academic substance of the disciplines. Concepts are the fundamental ideas of a discipline, and generalizations comprise the relationships among concepts. Bruner and his colleagues also stressed modes of inquiry within a discipline as being a proper object of study for students at all levels of education. Students should be led to inquire as scientists, for example, to come to an understanding of concepts and generalizations in the academic discipline of science. Students studying history should use the mode of inquiry that a historian uses to investigate specific events in history. Therefore, Process Oriented Education stressed inquiry learning as a means for students to acquire the structure of disciplines.

The notion of a spiral curriculum was also espoused by Bruner. A spiral curriculum is one where students encounter the same subject (and its concepts and generalizations) throughout their schooling. However, at each progressive encounter the concepts are broadened so that a student expands upon prior learning and expands the notion of the structure of the discipline. A typical example is found when students study American history in the 4th, 8th, and 12th grades.

During the 1960s, the U.S. Office of Education and the National Science Foundation sponsored massive curriculum development programs based on Bruner's hypothesis. School Mathematics Study Group (SMSG) mathematics programs, for example, introduced *new math* that stressed understanding the concepts that undergird mathematics operations. Biological Sciences Curriculum Study (BSCS) was an example of a new high school biology program that stressed inquiry-oriented learning. Man: A Course of Study (MACOS) reflected the new approach to social studies. Virtually every professional organization (e.g., National Council for Social Studies) was engaged in developing new curricula to reflect the values expressed by Bruner in *The Process of Education*. One of the major stumbling blocks to implementing process-oriented curricula was that they failed to provide adequate teacher training or effective ways to assess student learning and communicate the results to parents and the community.

Also during the 1960s, the Eastern Regional Institute for Education (ERIE), formerly the Regional Educational Laboratory of the U.S. Office of Education and located in Syracuse, New York, attempted to develop missing components of the new process-oriented curricula. ERIE helped school districts in upper New York State and western Pennsylvania adopt or adapt the new curricula. Process Oriented Education (Cole, 1973), as the movement came to be known, had a rather short life span in American education. Generally, only math and science teachers were fortunate enough to be enrolled in the National Science Foundation (NSF) sponsored intensive training programs and had the background knowledge and skills to implement the new curricula. Obviously, all of the nation's math and science teachers could not be involved in this critical training. Further, many of the programs lacked a clear statement of learning outcomes that could be communicated effectively to parents. Parents of elementary school students began to complain that their children could no longer add, subtract, multiply, and divide, and the parents themselves did not understand the language of the new mathematics.

An important part of the legacy of the Process Oriented Education movement was that schools needed to promote in children the tool skills of learning how to learn, which include the ability to read, write, compute, and problem solve (the scientific method). Additionally, the movement's great emphasis on meaning making as the primary task of learning set the stage for further research and development work in cognitive science and curriculum development. The concept of meaning making (the ability of students to construct meaning from experience) as the main focus of student learning and its emphasis on student reconstruction of experience also reinforced the philosophical orientation of John Dewey (see Chapter 2). The emphasis on meaning making was also clearly an outgrowth of the research of Jean Piaget.

Inquiry Learning, Verbal Reception Learning, and Intuitive Thinking

Process-oriented curricula emphasized discovery or inquiry learning. Discovery learning is closely aligned with the concept of process curricula that emphasized the structure of the disciplines and their mode of inquiry. Bruner (1961) asserts that in discovery learning the learner becomes the organizer of his own knowledge. It was generally held by Bruner and others that an emphasis on discovery learning in the schools would have the following desirable outcomes: (a) an increase of intellectual potency, (b) a shift from extrinsic to intrinsic rewards, (c) a mastery of the heuristics of discovery, and (d) the development of long-term memory. It was also widely held that discovery learning would significantly increase the motivation to learn. Some psychologists made a point of differentiating between discovery and inquiry learning (Suchman, 1962). Also, a distinction was made between discovery and guided discovery. In the latter, the student would be carefully guided to make meaning in order to maximize the time used to reach the criterion. Research by Gagne and Brown (1961), Gagne and Smith (1965), Kittell (1957), and others found that requiring students to verbalize reasons for their actions while engaging in inquiry learning facilitated the discovery of principles. Ausubel (1963), however, asserted that before a child could discover concepts and generalizations efficiently the educational problem must be structured, the materials and procedures arranged, and the learning environment organized in such a way that the discovery of a concept or generalization was inevitable.

This brief review of learning theory and research during the 1960s is intended to convey that the process oriented curricula of the 1960s emphasized meaning making as the main business of schooling. The hypotheses and research findings directly influenced the design and development of new curricula in a very comprehensive way during that decade.

The concept of verbal reception learning that supports didactic instruction is the opposite of inquiry or discovery learning. Verbal reception learning (Ausubel, 1963) is characterized by instruction that presents to students the entire content of the subject matter to be learned in final form. The role of the student is to understand and internalize the information so that it can be used at a later date. Meaningful learning, in this sense, requires that the learner subsume information into a formal cognitive structure. Meaningful learning is differentiated from rote learning or passive learning. Meaningful learning requires that the student have a sufficient experience background to relate information to a formal cognitive structure. Rote learning calls for the student to internalize verbatim material as a discrete end in itself; rote learning may not be related to a cognitive structure (Ausubel, 1963).

Verbal reception learning is related to discovery learning in the following way. For a student to be able to inquire in a specific academic discipline, some basic knowledge of that discipline is needed. Meaningful verbal reception learning uses advanced organizers so that students have a basis for incorporating new learning into a formal cognitive structure (Ausubel, 1963). Basic information acquired through verbal reception learning becomes the "grist for the mill" as students begin to engage in guided discovery learning to attain new insights or understandings with regard to a specific academic discipline.

Bruner (1960) also introduced the concept of intuitive learning as a vital component of Process Oriented Education. Intuitive thinking differs from inquiry or discovery learning processes. The latter proceed from well-defined steps and build toward a conclusion. On the other hand, the intuitive thinker uses short cuts to the solution of problems without an explicit awareness, initially, as to how the solution was reached. Bruner describes intuitive thinking as follows:

> Usually intuitive thinking rests on familiarity with the domain of knowledge involved and with its structure, which makes it possible for the thinker to leap about, skipping steps and employing short cuts in a manner that requires later rechecking of conclusions by more analytic means, whether deductive or inductive. (p. 58)

In general, intuitive thinking is less systematic than inductive thinking. Educational processes that promote the structure of an academic discipline may tend to promote intuitive thinking if the learning environment supports students in taking risks. However, if the emphasis in classroom instruction is on the right answer, developing the habit of intuitive thinking will probably be inhibited. In the next section, we explore the growth of cognitive science research which began about the same time as the Process Oriented Education movement was under way.

Cognitive Science Research in the Classrooms:
1970s to the Present

While the Process Oriented Education movement was being implemented in the 1960s another movement was under way that was to significantly influence learning related to schooling. During the late 1950s and the 1960s, the work of four researchers—Noam Chomsky, George Miller, Herbert Simon, and Alan Newell—built the platform for cognitive science. Chomsky proposed a theory of transformational grammar that explained our use of language. He argued, contrary to the behaviorist psychologists of the day, that our use of unobservable mental symbol structures determines how we think and how we store and use knowledge through the use of language. George Miller introduced the notion of the mind's ability to aggregate chunks of information that form the basis for information processing. Allan Newell and Herbert Simon initiated work in artificial intelligence that dealt with information processing. Newell and Simon's work, which began with the study of the computer's ability to process information, ultimately led to their studies of human problem solving as being similar to that of the computer (Bruer, 1993).

Newell and Simon (1972) studied how experts and novices engaged in problem solving in various academic disciplines. They discovered that experts have a breadth of knowledge in a specific academic domain, whereas novices do not. The study of domains of knowledge approximates the courses of study (e.g., mathematics, science) that comprise the process of schooling.

Newell and Simon's book *Human Problem Solving* provided the theoretical outlook and research methods that guide the work of cognitive science researchers to the present day (Bruer, 1993). The underlying assumption that guides current cognitive science research is that learning is problem solving. That is, the process of education should enable children and youths to learn to gather and process information that will become organized into stable mental structures to assist them in problem solving (Bruer, 1993, p. 12). The goal of cognitive science researchers, then, is to discover ways in which they can structure learning experiences so that novice learners can become experts within specific knowledge domains. In the sections that follow, highlights of the research are presented as they relate to instructional methods used in elementary schools, secondary schools, and colleges. The work to be cited is summarized in an important book by John Bruer (1993) titled *Schools for Thought: A Science of Learning in the Classroom.*

Cognitive scientists believe that the way humans process information is similar to the way that computers do. These learning theorists and researchers study the way that the mind processes symbols, organizes those symbols in storage (short- and-long term memory), and uses them to solve problems. Researchers in this field use such concepts as cognitive architecture, schemata, and working memory to explain how the mind acquires and uses information to organize experience and guide behavior in solving problems. The goal of the cognitive scientist is to help us understand how children develop from naive perceptors of experience to learners who master the content of a specific subject matter domain and thus become experts (Bruer, 1993, p. 52).

Early notions about learning tended to view the mind as a "muscle" that if exercised sufficiently would become strong. Thus, the study of formal subjects such as Latin, Greek, logic, and learning how to parse sentence structure would help the mind grow stronger. The value often espoused was that strong minds could learn virtually anything. By the mid-1970s, however, cognitive scientists found that general strength of the mind, that is, domain-independent thinking skills or generalizable thinking skills, could not account for human expertise (Bruer, 1993, p. 52). Researchers found that learning in a domain-specific subject together with general thinking skills were necessary for students to learn effectively. They also found that educators needed to be concerned about how learning is structured for pupils as well as what we want pupils to learn. This new synthesis of domain-specific knowledge, general thinking skills, and structure of learning activities provides the basis for helping children become intelligent novices and ultimately expert learners.

Cognitive scientists talk about weak and strong methods of learning. Weak methods are general in nature, not specific to a given domain of knowledge. The teaching of general critical thinking skills is an example of a weak method because it is not tied to thinking in a specific knowledge domain. That is not to say that general critical thinking skills are useless. However, to be useful they must be used in conjunction with domain-specific thinking skills. On the other hand, situation-specific or domain-specific methods of learning are strong. The concepts of strong and weak methods came from studies of expert knowledge. Results of research studies demonstrated again and again that "experts had better memories for items in their area of expertise, but not for items in general" (Bruer, 1993, p. 60). Domain-specific knowledge does contribute to one's ability to solve problems in that domain. One message for teachers from this research is that training in general study skills, for example, will not help students master knowledge in a specific field such as social studies. Skills specific to the study of social studies, however, are more likely to help students master knowledge in that field.

Children need to be taught to think about thinking as they go about the daily tasks of learning. The concept of metacognition, the ability to reflect on one's thinking and to be consciously aware of how one solves problems, is central to becoming an expert in a specific knowledge domain. In addition to being aware about one's thought processes, an expert learner is able to monitor and adjust thinking processes to expedite learning and problem solving. Bruer (1993) describes metacognitive processes as follows:

> Just as there are basic math and reading skills, there are basic metacognitive skills. Among the basic metacognitive skills are the abilities to predict the results of one's own problem-solving actions, to check the results of one's own actions (Did it work?), to monitor one's progress toward a solution (How am I doing?), and to test how reasonable one's actions and solutions are against the larger reality (Does this make sense?). (p. 72)

Cognitive scientists have found that metacognitive skills are domain-specific rather than general in nature. However, to become an expert in a specific domain one needs domain-specific knowledge, metacognitive skills, and general thinking strategies. What does this mean for educational practice? It may seem somewhat simplistic to say that students need educational experiences that provide them with higher-order thinking skills in specific academic fields but that is exactly what cognitive scientists recommend for schools to practice. Higher-order thinking, according to the new synthesis in cognitive science, requires that a student possess extensive knowledge in a specific domain to be able to solve problems in that domain. Chipman (1992), for example, points out that students need factual and procedural knowledge in specific domains and they need to know when to use this knowledge. In addition, students need to be able to metacognitively control the evolution of their problem-solving behavior. For students to ultimately be experts in a given knowledge domain, they need to acquire higher-order skills in what Resnick (1986) calls the enabling domains: mathematics, science, reading, and writing.

In the sections that follow, we review some of the highlights of cognitive science applied to classroom instruction. These descriptions review the joint work of classroom teachers and cognitive scientists in mathematics, science, reading, and writing.

Domain-Specific Knowledge in Mathematics

For a student to progress from a novice to an expert in school mathematics requires both conceptual and procedural knowledge. The link between concepts and procedures must be explicit if children are to perceive math as meaningful. Children need to understand the concept of number before they can understand procedures that use numbers. For multiple-digit subtraction to be meaningful, for example, a student needs to be able to combine substantive knowledge of number concepts and procedural knowledge of subtraction. If a student demonstrates procedural knowledge that does not mean that he or she has conceptual knowledge. Instruction for students needs to make explicit the relationships between conceptual and procedural knowledge. The issue is described as follows:

> Most school math does not do this. Instruction either doesn't teach the underlying representations (such as the mental number line and the part-whole schema) or doesn't make the link between concept and procedure explicit. Some children make the connection on their own, but many do not. Without the link, mathematics is meaningless. (Bruer, 1993, p. 99)

Solving problems using mathematics is typically difficult for most school children. Cognitive scientists have worked on this issue by helping children learn to pose problems. The staff of Vanderbilt University's Learning Technology Center combined videodisc technology and cognitive science to produce *Adventures of Jasper Woodbury* as an instructional method to teach problem-solving skills to middle school students. "Jasper" provides invitations to thinking as students are presented with exciting video contexts that are the basis for creating and solving mathematical problems. To solve problems, students must analyze all the available information in the visual presentation and engage in multistep problem solving to address the dilemmas presented to them in the video.

Results from research comparing "Jasper" students with control groups reveal that "Jasper" students are more competent at solving problems and also have a higher degree of interest in mathematics and mathematics problem solving. The "Jasper" network now serves 1,500 students in more than nine states (Bruer, 1993, p. 110).

John Anderson, a professor at Carnegie Mellon University, applied cognitive science principles to high school geometry. His Geometry Proof Tutor (GPT) provided the means of delivering a year-long instructional program in geometry to 10th-grade students. GPT is an interactive computer-assisted instructional system that uses an underlying expert model as the basis for instructional sequences. Anderson uses a theory called ACT, which asserts that all knowledge begins as factual knowledge. He then theorizes that we use factual knowledge stored in declarative memory by using domain-independent methods such as means-to-end analysis. Anderson believes that as learners use factual knowledge to solve problems their cognitive structure produces new domain-specific rules that enable them to move toward being expert learners.

The movement from facts to domain-specific rules is illustrated by the following example of finding the price of an item at a store after taking a 20% discount and then adding an 8% sales tax:

IF the goal is to find the price after a 20 % discount

THEN multiply the price by .80.

IF the goal is to find the price including the sales tax

THEN multiply the price by 1.08.

After repeated use, composition collapses these two rules into one:

IF the goal is to find the price after a 20 % discount but with the 8 % sales tax

THEN multiply the price by .864. (Bruer, 1993, p. 114)

Anderson and his colleagues developed the tutoring system to provide a set of expert rules that students use to develop and correct factual knowledge. The computer tutor was designed to work in the way that a human tutor would work with a student to build more expert ways of dealing with the construction of geometry proofs. Anderson built the production rules for solving geometric problems by analyzing how experts in the field used knowledge to construct proofs. The purpose of the program is to help students see the structure and purpose of geometry proofs. Proofs are presented as a path on the computer monitor where the student moves from givens to the proof, with geometric justification provided for each step. Students learn that to construct a path they have to use definitions, postulates, and theorems in addition to their existing knowledge base. Basically, students learn rules and procedures with which to infer new knowledge. The computer tutor provides clues to students if they make the wrong production decision. They can correct their decision and enter a new one or ask for help. The computer gives students specific hints to get them back on the solution path. If students make persistent errors, the computer will solve the problem for them (Bruer, 1993, pp. 120-123).

Anderson and his colleagues analyzed the behavior of students as they progressed throughout the year-long course in geometry. The GPT helped weak students the most; bright but low-achieving students also responded well to the program. Students of average ability who lacked confidence in their math skills also benefited significantly from the GPT. Among other interesting findings were the following:

> Strong students spent more time at the outset planning a proof. These students developed a global plan before they touched the keyboard, but once they had started they completed the proofs quickly. Weak students used the given information to begin making inferences immediately without developing a strategic plan. (Bruer, 1993, p. 124)

Domain-Specific Knowledge in Science

Learning in science depends on prior knowledge built into long-term memory. Bruer (1993) points out that "effective science instruction has to be sensitive to how long term memory works. All learning depends on prior knowledge. Learners actively construct understanding by relating current experience, including classroom instruction, to preexisting schemata stored in long term memory" (p. 131). The problem that science teachers encounter is that children often have acquired a great deal of information related to how the physical world works. However, this information tends to be fragmentary, unintegrated, and not easily applied to problem solving. The job of the science teacher is to help students organize information into knowledge and guide them to use it in creating solutions to science-related problems that they encounter in the science classroom.

To move students from novice to expert in science requires that teachers help them gain knowledge and skill in scientific reasoning. Three kinds of knowledge and representation are involved in scientific reasoning. These representations, according to Bruer (1993), are (a) everyday knowledge, or naive schemata, (b) scientific reasoning knowledge, or expert schemata, and (c) formal equations, or mathematical versions of expert schemata. The expert has all three kinds of representations, whereas the novice usually has only the first and third. Unfortunately for novice learners, little help is offered to help them bridge the gap between naive schemata and formal equations. Thus, many students learn to manipulate equations mechanically and solve problems without understanding what they are doing; that is, they lack the conceptual structures to make explicit connections between the equations and the structures. Bruer (1993) notes, for example, that physics courses don't require that students learn physics. This allows students to "get through" high school and college physics without ever understanding the domain-specific cognitive structures that would enable them to gain meaning from their studies (p. 151).

A Theory of Instruction
Emerging From Cognitive Science

From work with students in mathematics and science, cognitive scientists have evolved a tentative theory of instruction. The theory includes the following postulates: (a) learning should be anchored in the everyday experience of students; (b) active problem solving is preferable to rote mastery of facts; (c) transfer is more likely to occur if learning takes place in contexts similar to those in which the knowledge should be used; and (d) instruction should involve group discussion that makes reasoning explicit and overt (Bruer, 1993, pp. 157-159). The instructional process stated above also implicitly includes the key features of the scientific method which are asking questions, performing experiments, formulating laws, observing the generalization of laws, and revising laws.

The theory stated above should be applied to domain-specific learning in math and science. The theory may also have implications for the teaching of reading and writing skills, which are the tool skills for learning in a specific knowledge domain. The next two sections deal with advances made in the teaching of reading and writing based on learning research.

Reading: The Cornerstone of Cognitive Competence

Reading is a complex cognitive task. Clearly, it is one of the key tool skills of learning. The ability to unlock meaning from the printed page is vital to the education of children and youths. The research conducted by cognitive scientists to date demonstrates clearly that a skilled reader relies on knowledge stored in long-term memory to construct meaning from text. Reading starts with recognizing word meaning and then proceeds to an understanding of phrases and clauses. Sentence meaning results from the integration of smaller units. Researchers who use the methods of cognitive science (e.g., Beck & Carpenter, 1986) inform us that readers move from integrating small units to building the representation of a total text in which the readers achieve a gist of what they have read and store the gist in long-term memory.

A significant contribution of research in reading has been to underscore the importance of automaticity—speed and accuracy—in word recognition. The research indicated that word recognition, although not sufficient to ensure fluent reading, forms the basis for eventual expertise in reading ability. Automaticity is a critical early reading skill and is the prerequisite for ultimate efficient reading. Most researchers in the field of reading agree that the essentials of effective reading comprehension are that the reader (a) understands that the purpose of reading is to construct meaning, (b) activates relevant background knowledge to gain meaning from printed text, (c) allocates attention to concentrate on major content ideas, (d) evaluates the constructed meaning (gist) for internal consistency with prior knowledge and common sense, (e) tests inferences, and (f) monitors all of the above to see if comprehension is occurring (Bruer, 1993, p. 206).

Writing: Transforming Knowledge

Research on classroom instruction in writing has advanced significantly in the past decade. Practical instructional techniques are now available to the conventional classroom teacher. Much of the research that has moved the field of writing forward has been conducted at Carnegie Mellon University by Linda Flower and John Hayes (see Bruer, 1993, pp. 215-250). Flower and Hayes have studied the writing process from the perspective of expert and novice writers and discovered that planning is the primary difference between both types of writers. The research evidence indicates that writers who produce highly rated texts do significantly more initial planning than those whose texts are not highly rated. The planning that differentiates good writers from poor writers is rhetorically oriented (as described below) rather than dealing with the content of the piece.

Skilled writers engage in constructive planning prior to writing. These writers tend to use a mind-set for writing that includes all the categories that the discipline of rhetoric requires. Rhetorical categories include identifying the key point of the message, specifying the purpose of the message, identifying the audience for the message, and using text convention to deliver the message. Skilled writers build a representation that places the content of their message in an audience-directed rhetorical framework.

To help students engage in constructive planning prior to writing, Flower developed a collaborative planning process used by students to visualize all aspects of a rhetorical plan. The Flower planning process requires two students to engage in discussion on a piece of writing, with one of the partners acting as the planner and the other as a supporter.

Another important finding with regard to writing in basic education deals with the issue of knowledge transmission and knowledge transformation. Knowledge telling is the kind of writing most often used in elementary and secondary schools. When engaged in knowledge-telling-writing, the student uses a "cue from the writing assignment to locate an item in long term memory, searches for content immediately around that item, puts that content onto a page and then stops writing" (Bruer, 1993, p. 219). The product of knowledge telling is often a piece of writing in which the sentences are correct, but there is no purpose, gist, or coherence to the message. It is as if the student has listed a chain of related information but with no integrating or rhetorical qualities. This technique of knowledge telling is, unfortunately, what most schools and colleges expect of students.

Skilled writers, on the other hand, are knowledge transformers. Scardamalia and Bereiter (1987) found from their research that expert writers tend to look at the content of a piece of writing from a rhetorical perspective. Because skilled writing takes audience and purpose into account, the content of a writing piece is not just telling knowledge but transforming it to meet the communication needs of the audience. If schools are to meet the goal of producing skilled writers, they must help students move from knowledge telling to knowledge transforming. To state it in a way that is consistent with the content of this chapter, students must make meaning of the content they wish to communicate and then pass it through a rhetorical screen in a collaborative planning process prior to beginning the writing task.

Principles of Learning

The Institute for Learning was established in 1996 at the Learning Research and Development Center at the University of Pittsburgh. Lauren Resnick, the Institute's director, has developed an approach to school improvement based on seven principles of learning culled from the past 20 years of research in cognitive science: effort-based education, clear expectations, academic rigor in a thinking curriculum, students as knowledge constructors, accountable talk, socializing intelligence, and learning as apprenticeship (Resnick, 1995). Each of these principles is discussed briefly below.

Effort-based education is based on the assumption that achievement is more a function of effort than exclusively a result of one's native ability. This assumption does not deny the influence of native ability and heredity, but it does state that effort to learn is more important.

A system organized for effort has four components that differ from traditional classroom practices (Rothman, 1996). First, students know what is expected. Second, fair and credible evaluation of student learning helps students and parents monitor progress toward the achievement of standards. Third, celebrating the achievement of standards rewards all students who work hard. Fourth, time will vary for individual students to master standards, but the results remain fixed.

Clear expectations are communicated to students through standards made available to and discussed with students. These standards become the visible benchmarks by which students can monitor and judge their own progress.

A thinking curriculum provides *academic rigor* for students. Students are expected to acquire important knowledge, use that knowledge to solve problems, use the knowledge and thinking skills to continue learning, and understand the differences between finished and corrected work and work in progress. "There is no thinking without knowledge, and there is no knowledge without thinking" (Rothman, 1996, p. 6).

Students as knowledge constructors must engage in *deep learning* to explore the major concepts and generalizations in academic disciplines and make meaning of them. Conceptual frameworks are used by students to organize the knowledge and skills that they learn.

Accountable talk improves students' thinking by encouraging them to use knowledge to create knowledge (Rothman, 1996, p. 9). Students learn to use evidence to support their arguments and to draw conclusions. Accountable talk is not idle conversation; it requires that students use standards of evidence and standards of reasoning appropriate to the subject matter. Teachers bear the primary responsibility to ensure that students' talk is accountable.

Socializing intelligence refers to the belief that all children have the right and the obligation to think and understand. "By treating all students as if they are smart, they will come to be smart" (Rothman, 1996, p. 10). This principle of learning is achieved by expecting students to analyze problems and ask good questions. In essence, acting as if children are intelligent creates the beliefs, strategies, and habits that constitute intelligence.

Learning as apprenticeship underscores the notion that powerful learning occurs when students participate in creating products for interested audiences, evaluate and revise work until it meets quality standards, work under people who have expertise in the learning task, and stretch beyond current capabilities by collaborating on complex tasks (Resnick, 1995).

Resnick and her colleagues are currently working with a number of school districts across the country to implement a comprehensive system of learning based on the seven principles described above. In doing so, Resnick is using the learning processes and the instructional techniques that have been demonstrated in cognitive research to make a significant difference in student learning. She and her colleagues, in collaboration with school districts, are integrating the academic and social policies and support structures that will promote comprehensive implementation of these seven principles of learning. The Institute is working with school districts to develop a comprehensive systemwide professional development program to enable teachers to implement the principles of learning in their classrooms and also is supporting principals in their efforts to exercise instructional leadership in their schools.

Concluding Comments About Learning Research

Over a period of decades, learning researchers have made a significant contribution to the improvement of basic and higher education. Perhaps the most comprehensive and significant advances that can be implemented immediately to improve educational practice are in the field of writing. The work of Flower and her colleagues (see Bruer, 1993) provides generalizable findings that can assist teachers to help students improve the quality of their writing. Some of the findings in reading also can be translated quite readily into practice in classrooms. However, most of the current work in mathematics and science relies on expensive video or computer equipment that makes the widespread dissemination of methods based on cognitive science not yet practical. Further, the development costs for sophisticated programs such as *Adventures of Jasper Woodbury* and GPT will limit the widespread development and dissemination of those programs that truly excite learners and promote the development of the conceptual understanding that undergirds mathematics and science.

Cognitive science is still in its infancy (Bruer, 1993). Its findings to date hold great promise for the future of American education. For that promise to be fulfilled, a stronger critical mass of findings easily translated into school practice has to emerge. Teacher training institutions will have to prepare the future generation of teachers to be ready to teach for conceptual understanding. Significant staff development training will also have to be provided to the thousands of teachers currently in the nation's schools.

The next section deals with the constructivist approach to teaching that is currently gaining the attention of many teachers in American schools. The basic tenets of the constructivist approach to teaching are consistent with instructional practices that promote active learning for pupils.

The Constructivist Approach
to Teaching and Learning

A recent surge of interest in a constructivist approach to teaching and learning provides additional emphasis on students making meaning of school experience. The 1993 book by Brooks and Brooks, *The Case for Constructivist Classrooms,* provides guiding principles for teachers and administrators who wish to embrace an approach to learning that actively engages students in the process.

The constructivist approach focuses on knowledge and learning and proposes pedagogical strategies that will help teachers guide students in acquiring new understandings about the world they encounter. A constructivist approach to learning is based, to a large extent, on the work of Piaget as described in Chapter 2. The essence of constructivism is captured by Brooks and Brooks (1993) as follows:

> It sounds like a simple proposition: we construct our own understandings of the world in which we live. We search for tools to help us understand our experiences. To do so is human nature. . . . Each of us makes sense of our world by synthesizing new experiences in what we have previously come to understand. (p. 5)

The constructivist approach draws heavily on Piaget's notion of dynamic equilibrium in which the learner seeks to assimilate and accommodate new experience in previously developed cognitive structures. As learners experience situations in which they encounter a discrepancy between prior knowledge and new phenomena, they seek to resolve the discrepancy. The resolution of the discrepancy results in the creation of new knowledge for the learners.

Constructivist approaches to teaching (see Brooks & Brooks, 1993, p. 33) embrace the following principles:

- Posing problems of emerging relevance to students
- Structuring learning around primary concepts

- Seeking and valuing students' points of view
- Adapting curriculum to address students' suppositions
- Assessing student learning in the context of teaching

Each of these principles is discussed briefly below.

Posing problems of emerging relevance to students does not mean that learning is guided simply on the current interests of the children or youths. Rather, it means that teachers structure problems that are made relevant to students' interests on the basis of their current state of knowledge. The teacher mediates the classroom environment by posing problems to students that are within the range of their cognitive abilities, capturing their interest, and then guiding them toward a solution. The problems presented often have multiple perspectives, and teachers provide students with sufficient time and guidance to explore alternative solutions.

Structuring learning around primary concepts means that constructivists take a holistic approach to instruction. Constructivist teachers present a set of concepts as wholes and then engage students in breaking each whole into its relevant parts. Typical learning activities require students to compare and contrast and to analyze and reflect. Students are often engaged in classification activities as they break conceptual wholes into parts and then reconstruct them to gain greater understanding.

Seeking and valuing students' points of view is necessary for the constructivist teacher as a means of diagnosing the students' current level of knowledge. It is also important to help guide students to a perception of relevance to their emerging interests. "Students' points of view are windows into their reasoning" (Brooks & Brooks, 1993, p. 60). Listening carefully to students rather than just talking to them is an important principle of constructivist teaching.

Adapting curriculum to address students' suppositions builds on the previous three principles. Essentially, this principle is concerned with verifying the question that a student is currently asking about some topic of interest by identifying the mismatch between prior knowledge and current observations. Working with the perceived mismatch, the teacher structures experiences that deal with the student's questions and move the student in the direction of discovering appropriate relationships.

Assessing student learning in the context of teaching is consistent with the notions of authentic assessment discussed in Chapter 4. One essential principle is that assessment should be viewed as a verification of the student's current state of knowledge so that more appropriate learning experiences can be provided. This means that assessment is not just an accountability device but is also viewed as a natural part of the instructional process as teachers observe students working with others and with instructional materials as a means of verifying progress.

Brooks and Brooks (1993; pp. 101-118) propose a list of descriptors that help teachers consider how they would change their behavior to be consistent with constructivist principles:

- Encourage and accept student autonomy
- Use raw data and primary sources along with manipulative, interactive, and physical materials
- Use cognitive terminology such as classify, analyze, predict, and create when framing learning tasks
- Allow student responses to drive lessons, shift instructional strategies, and alter content
- Inquire about students' understandings of concepts before sharing their own understanding of those concepts
- Encourage students to engage in dialogue, both with the teacher and with one another
- Encourage student inquiry by asking thoughtful, open-ended questions and encouraging students to ask questions of each other
- Seek elaboration of students' initial responses
- Engage students in experiences that might engender contradictions to their initial hypotheses and then encourage discussion
- Allow wait time after posing questions
- Provide time for students to construct relationships and create metaphors
- Nurture students' natural curiosity through frequent use of the learning cycle model

The behaviors listed above for constructivist teaching are similar to those described for authentic instruction, process-oriented instruction, or inquiry-oriented instruction. They are not new to education. What is important to note, however, is that their roots are explicitly tied to a theory of knowledge and learning that emanates from the work of Piaget, Bruner, and other cognitive psychologists. The behavioral descriptors are also consistent with the philosophical orientation of John Dewey and the neopragmatists (see Chapter 2). For teachers and schools to adopt constructivist principles means that they must create new classroom cultures that differ from the traditional classroom culture. The major thesis of the constructivist approach is that learners are active inquirers who construct meaning from past and present experience. And in so doing, they develop attitudes and dispositions that will promote the habit of lifelong learning.

Summary

The purpose of this chapter has been to provide the reader with an understanding of how learning theory and research have a direct influence on one's vision of educational processes and outcomes. Learning is what schooling is all about, after all. The integrated model presented in this book (see Chapter 5) holds that one's vision of education directly influences instruction designed to implement that vision. Further, the model posits that support conditions must be provided to assist the implementation of the vision's instructional model. The ultimate evaluation or assessment of the outcomes of one's vision requires that instructional strategies and support conditions be internally consistent. Assessment also requires multiple sources of data to provide for a comprehensive analysis of educational processes and outcomes in relation to the postulates of one's vision.

The chapter began with a review of the influence of 1960s' learning theory on significant changes implemented in American schools. The influence of Jerome Bruner's (1960) book *The Process of Education* was described. Bruner and his fellow cognitive psychologists had a significant influence on the development and implementation of Process Oriented Education that attempted to alter classroom practice in American schools. The influence of that program was somewhat blunted by the fact that insufficient attention was given to the professional development needs of teachers. The lack of sufficient assessment devices to authenticate and report student achievement also hampered its widespread implementation. It is interesting to note, however, that the current model of authenticity in instruction, assessment, and student work (Newmann, Wehlage, & Lamborn, 1992) is highly consistent with Process Oriented Education. The constructivist approach to teaching and learning, described in this chapter, also embraces many of the process-oriented principles (Brooks & Brooks, 1993).

The second most important development in learning theory and research in the last half of the 20th century has been the work of cognitive scientists. John Bruer's (1993) book *Schools for Thought* summarizes the important advances of cognitive science on learning in the classroom. The important difference between cognitive science learning and Process Oriented Education and constructivism is that cognitive science learning emerges from classroom-based research, whereas the propositions of Process Oriented Education and constructivism are based primarily on theory; as yet, no comprehensive research base exists to support these theories. The principles of learning proposed by Resnick are a distillation of the body of cognitive science research, and the principles are expressed so that they have direct application to classroom practices.

The recent influence of constructivism on educational practice reflects the seminal work of Jean Piaget. It is interesting to note that the three approaches to instruction described in this chapter (Process Oriented Education, cognitive science learning, and constructivism) all embrace the notion that meaning making is both the primary process and the outcome of education. Meaning making as an instructional strategy and as an outcome criterion requires that students be primarily engaged in active, as opposed to passive, learning and that classroom learning environments foster a constructivist approach to teaching and learning.

4

Understanding
Moral Leadership in a
Learning Organization
The Third Step

A school is an organization whose principal purpose is learning. While that may appear to be a truism, any close observer of school organizations can readily see that a school or a school district fulfills different purposes for different participants. In many areas, school districts are the largest single employer. Accordingly, the school is viewed by some as valuable for its employment opportunities. In other instances, especially in a society with an increasing number of either single parents or households where both parents are fully employed, the school fulfills a significant custodial or child-care function. Still, we maintain that a school is primarily a learning organization. It exists to educate those who want to learn. As such, educational leadership needs to be understood in terms that constitute a vision of the learning needs of its principal clients—students.

The work of two authors, Peter Senge and Thomas Sergiovanni, stands out in the search for a meaningful basis for the learning school. In each case, they provide fresh insight into the role of leadership in today's institutions. Peter Senge develops a theory of shared leadership for a learning organization that uses a systems perspective. Most significant for the learning school, Senge provides a rationale for shared leadership. Each of the elements of Senge's outlook will be dealt with in turn. Thomas Sergiovanni articulates a second major theory that seeks a basis for authority in leadership, with emphasis on its moral grounding. Recall that moral questions about knowing and learning were left open in Chapter 2; Sergiovanni's approach to leadership fills that void. In both cases, we explicate a vision of educational leadership for the future.

Vision Beyond Linear Thinking

The future direction of schools will be based on perceiving patterns of change. There is a need to develop mental models for decision making that transcend the problem of *linear thinking* (Senge, 1990). Linear thinking tends to deal with problems as if they can be approached in sequence. That is, one deals with a series of problems as if they had already been placed in some priority order. But when one confronts a complex problem, such as school reform, the issue of priorities has not been settled. As a consequence, it becomes necessary to identify and relate all of the problematic features to deal with the problem. An organization's statement of vision needs to deliberately account for the interrelationship of these features. Furthermore, all stakeholders in an organization must share the vision for the entire organization to work toward its fulfillment.

For Peter Senge (1990), a "shared vision is not an idea. . . . [It] is, rather, a force in people's hearts" (p. 206). Senge continues, "It may be inspired by an idea but . . . if it is compelling enough to acquire the support of more than one person—then it is no longer an abstraction. It is palpable" (p. 206). In simplest terms, the question is a matter of what we want to create and achieve.

It is important to note here that a vision once shared can lead to common aspiration and a sense of connectedness among stakeholders. Senge makes a crucial distinction in noting that a vision of one person or one group within an organization when imposed on the whole elicits, at best, reluctant conformity without real commitment: "A vision is truly shared when you and I have a similar picture and are committed to one another having it, not just to each of us, individually, having it" (p. 206). As such, shared vision leads to common commitment. Herein lies our emphasis on shared vision in educational leadership.

When asked in an interview whether most schools can be considered learning institutions, Senge responded,

Definitely not. A learning organization is an organization in which people at all levels are, collectively, continually enhancing their capacity to create things they really want to create. And most of the educators I talk with don't feel like they're doing this. Most teachers feel oppressed trying to conform to all kinds of rules, goals, and objectives, many of which they don't believe in. Teachers don't work together; there's very little sense of collective learning going on in most schools. (quoted in O'Neil, 1995, p. 20)

One could question how true a picture this is of most schools. But in our experience, Senge's representation is on the mark. As Ernest Boyer (1983) pointed out in his study of American secondary schools, "teachers feel isolated. The combination of the self-contained classroom and a heavy teaching schedule gives teachers few opportunities to share common problems or sustain an intellectual life" (p. 158). Under such circumstances, the opportunities to share vision are nonexistent.

Obviously, some changes in the structure of schools need to be made. As Senge suggests, "we need to find ways to get teachers really working together; we need to create an environment where they can continually reflect on what they are doing and learn more and more what it takes to work in teams" (quoted in O'Neil, 1995, p. 20). Part of the problem, according to Senge, is the tendency to fragment knowledge into separate specialized pieces without an overarching and integrative vision. In this regard, it is noteworthy that Abraham Maslow late in his career studied high-performing teams and concluded that shared vision was central to performance. What Maslow had observed was that for the individual in such teams the task at hand could not be separated from the organization's overall purpose (Senge, 1990, p. 208).

To summarize at this point in the analysis, one cannot have a learning school without shared vision. Without a pull toward some goal that participants truly want to achieve, the forces supporting the status quo can be overwhelming. With shared vision one is more likely to expose accustomed ways of thinking and redefine them in cooperative terms, thereby recognizing personal and organizational shortcomings. A linear view of problem solving that approaches problems in serial fashion reinforces a fragmented notion of knowledge and thus fails to grasp the big picture of what is at stake. Furthermore, developing a collective vision need not be some mysterious enterprise entered into by a chosen few. It requires discipline to bring together personal competencies of individuals with a clear sense of sharing an organization's goals, objectives, and long-range aspirations.

The Systems Perspective

It is apparent that linear thinking is not useful when creating shared vision. A systems perspective notes that the structure of an organization tends to lead to certain outcomes. The structure of an organization has a pervasive influence on the performance of individuals in that system. To understand an organization it is necessary to comprehend its structural influences, to look beyond personalities and events and identify *underlying structures* that shape individual action. As Donella Meadows observed, "A truly profound and different insight is the way you begin to see that the system causes its own behavior" (quoted in Senge, 1990, p. 43).

The term *structure* means the key interrelations that influence behavior over time. The relations within a system are not simply relations among participants but extend to include such key variables as total population served (i.e., clients of the system) and the managerial know-how within the system.

In Senge's view, individuals within such systems are not absolved of responsibility even though the variables of the system are above and beyond individual control. He notes that, even though structural influence on individual behavior is subtle, individuals with a systems outlook can find ways to alter the structure within which they work. In some instances, individuals may have no other alternative than to reject the system's structure. Consequently, the system undergoes a crisis or turning point when a revision, that is a re-visioning, needs to occur.

An example that Senge (1990) provides comes from industry but is nonetheless illuminating. He points out that for years the Big Three automakers in Detroit relied on a mental model that the American consumer based their purchase of automobiles on styling. Quality and reliability were not viewed as motivating factors in car buying. Market forces changed, and as Japanese and German automobiles were more intensively marketed in the United States, consumer choice changed to a greater emphasis on overall quality and reliability. Over time the market share of foreign cars purchased in the United States approached 38% by 1986. General Motors, in particular, was forced to face the realization that its mental model of styling as the key factor was flawed and would have to be revised. Earlier corporate leaders had been unaware of their own mental model about styling; thus their production objectives remained unchanged. Only the crisis of diminishing market share forced them to rethink their mental model.

Similarly, educators have mental models of the school which may be outdated and dysfunctional. Here again Senge's comment is apropos:

> Educational institutions are designed and structured in a way that reinforces the idea that my job as a teacher is as an individual teaching *my* kids. I have literally heard teachers say, "When I close that classroom door, I'm God in my universe." This focus on the individual is so deeply embedded in our culture that it's very hard for people to even see it. (quoted in O'Neil, 1995, p. 21)

When the school is understood in systems terms, what happens in individual classrooms, by themselves, is insufficient. What happens in one classroom with one teacher needs to be related to all others. Is the learning in one classroom counterproductive to the learning in another? Do they complement one another? Is the way that meaning making is advanced in social studies or literature related to that in natural science? Not that they should be held in strict methodological conformity, but the qualitative methods of investigation in the social sciences and literature should be related to the quantitative approaches in natural sciences. The relationship between these is crucial to a learning school. In short, if the school is viewed as a *learning organization*, such questions are central to its vision. Furthermore, its vision does not consist of statements issued from on high (i.e., from a principal or from the central office) but are truly shared by all participants in the system.

The Learning Organization

The development of a learning organization, consistent with our focus on a learning school, requires discipline. Senge (1990) identifies five disciplinary elements that are critical for the kind of sharing required in an enterprise based on mutual learning. These elements are personal mastery, mental models, shared vision, team learning, and systems thinking.

Personal Mastery

Mastery is not a fixed state. Instead, it is a product of one's constant striving for higher and higher levels of proficiency. Illustrations from the arts come to mind. Over time the work of Pablo Picasso gives evidence of significant changes in artistic impressions of both a social and a spiritual perception of reality. The musical work of virtuosos like Luciano Pavarotti, Placido Domingo, YoYo Ma, or Wynton Marsalis exhibits constant growth. Such artists have committed themselves to an ever greater vision of their art. In Senge's (1990) terms,

> Personal mastery is the discipline of continually clarifying and deepening our personal vision, of focusing our energies, of developing patience, and of seeing reality objectively. As such, it is an essential cornerstone of the learning organization—the learning organization's spiritual foundation. An organization's commitment to and capacity for learning can be no greater than that of its members. (p. 7)

Unfortunately, many organizations do not promote such growth in personal mastery. Many teachers entering the profession are highly motivated. Yet after 10 years of service, despite programs for so-called staff development, they end their careers by just putting in their time.

Mental Models

Mental models, as we have seen, are frequently unconscious assumptions that influence the working of an organization. We refer the reader to the previous two chapters as a basis for identifying mental models. Educators must ask themselves what mental models they carry in professional activity about knowledge, about teaching and learning, about organizational behavior, and about leadership. The task is to identify the often unstated assumptions on which behavior in an organization is based. Senge's (1990) analysis is informative:

> The discipline of working with mental models starts with turning the mirror inward; learning to unearth our internal pictures of the world to bring them to the surface and hold them rigorously to scrutiny. It also includes the ability to carry on "learningful" conversations that balance inquiry and advocacy, where people expose their own thinking effectively and make that thinking open to the influence of others. (p. 9)

As seen in the earlier example of General Motors Corporation during the 1980s, such thinking about mental models was distinctly absent. To lead a learning school, educators must determine whether they are similarly unaware of the mental models that guide their day-to-day behavior.

Shared Vision

Shared vision has the power to bind people in an organization together around a common identity and sense of destiny. Where a vision is shared, individual actors in an organization learn and excel not because they are told to but because they want to.

Many teachers with a personal vision for an organization never see it translated into practice because they do not share it and open it for wider scrutiny among other organizational members. The business pages of newspapers are replete with organizational leaders who have been supplanted because they did not share their vision for the organization they led. But where a vision is shared, Senge (1990) notes, not as a "cookbook" but as "a set of principles and guiding practices," then the vision has power for the organization (p. 9).

Team Learning

For Senge, dialogue is crucial among organizational members. He stresses that dialogue is not competitive thinking or seeing which ideas win but, rather, the cooperative enterprise of thinking together. Accordingly, team learning, when taken together with the other four disciplines, constitutes a way of effective organizational development and leadership.

Systems Thinking

We have already referred to systems thinking in the previous section of this chapter. In summary, organizations of human endeavor constitute systems of coordinated and interrelated actions. In contrast to focusing on individual facets of large systems, systems thinking considers the big picture. As such, systems thinking looks at the overall conceptual framework of a human enterprise to uncover its subtle patterns of action. In turn, such a worldview enables organizational members to change structure and consequent behavior.

These five disciplines describe the five components of a learning organization. By discipline, Senge means a body of theory and technique to be studied and mastered and then be put into practice. It is vital for the five disciplines to develop as an ensemble. Systems thinking is the discipline that integrates the other four. Hence, systems thinking is what he calls the *fifth discipline*.

These five disciplines are relevant to a learning school. As Senge notes, "You can make pretty compelling arguments that systems thinking, building a shared vision, dialogue, and learning how to reflect on our mental models are, at some level, educational undertakings more than business undertakings" (quoted in O'Neil, 1995, p. 23).

Furthermore, school reform efforts that focus on the need for changing the ways schools go about learning require not a random selection of immediately pressing problems but a holistic approach to a complex of interrelated problems. A learning school requires nothing less than such a visioning process.

Of course, it might be argued that what works in business enterprises, where Senge developed his ideas, will not necessarily work in schools. Just as government institutions—including the interplay among legislatures, courts, and executive agencies—are distinct from a for-profit corporation, so are schools. Senge recognizes that: "Innovation in education really is much more challenging than it is in business, because educators have . . . multiple constituencies" (quoted in O'Neil, 1995, p. 23).

Sources of Authority

The emphasis in Senge's thought is on a learning organization. A complement to this organizational theory is found in the analysis of leadership by Thomas J. Sergiovanni, who notes that discussion about attitudes and values inform the role of the leader. At the same time, there is talk of leadership being shared with emphasis placed on the content of education. Sergiovanni (1992) adds to what he calls this "new kind of leadership" by providing a moral basis (p. 1). Earlier, it was noted that the moral question for educational leadership needs to be addressed. Sergiovanni's position in this regard uniquely stands out in the educational administration literature.

He begins his analysis by posing questions not about leadership but about followership. *Who* should one follow? *What* should one follow, and *why*? The *who* one follows, in traditional management terms, is a designated leader. The *what* one follows is the leader's vision or where there is no articulated vision, some standard practice is followed. The "why" question is typically answered by a leader's ability to manipulate followers. Sergiovanni notes that many leaders prefer not to answer the "why" question because they expect their position and the power it represents to be a sufficient answer. Accordingly, the simplest way to answer any of the questions is to rely on bureaucratic authority. As such, *follow-me* leadership calls upon followership by virtue of the leader's position.

There are, however, alternatives to this authoritarian leadership style. A psychologically based approach suggests that people follow a leader because of the rewards the leader can dispense. The leader provides a pleasant environment or the leader presents a pleasing personality. The technical-rational proficiency of a leader may convince followers that the leader knows more or knows better than others. Sergiovanni does not deny validity for such bases for authority in leadership, but none of them is wholly sufficient. He notes that each style of leadership can elicit followers for very different reasons.

As his analysis continues, Sergiovanni (1992) looks at the advantages and disadvantages of each approach. In his estimation, bureaucratic authority is overemphasized in schools. He rejects sole reliance on psychologically based leadership because it requires teachers and parents to respond to a leader's personality, which is not a fully adequate justification for the leader's role. Its inadequacy lies in a notion of personality that is, at best, elusive and makes leadership style, not content, central to administrative leadership. We concur with Sergiovanni that both style and content in leadership are of equal importance.

Moral Leadership

Moral leadership is based on felt obligations and duties derived from widely shared professional and community values, ideas, and ideals. To accomplish these goals we need to create learning communities within schools. The norms and values associated with professionalism and the norms and values that define the school as a learning community can then become substitutes for "follow me" leadership. Sergiovanni's (1992) version of moral leadership, based on the learning community, is strikingly related to Senge's (1990) espousal of the learning organization. Sergiovanni adds the morality element to Senge's fifth discipline. Senge seems to argue for the learning organization based on a technical-rational argument, but Sergiovanni argues that the learning community demonstrates a moral force that enhances the legitimacy of the leader's authority.

Sergiovanni compares two metaphors of the school: (a) instructional delivery systems and (b) the learning community. He argues that the instructional delivery system concept requires teachers and administrators to follow scripts. In these circumstances, people are dependent on external motivation and monitoring for their actions. For this reason, instructional delivery systems are management intensive and interpersonal leadership intensive.

If the school is viewed as a learning community, however, the issues that come to mind are very different. Stakeholders have to focus on the shared values, purposes, and commitments that bond the community together; how teachers, parents, and students can work together to embody these values; and what kinds of obligations to the community members should have and how these obligations will be enforced. The image of the learning community is based on very different assumptions and legitimizing factors than the instructional delivery system.

Systemic Sharing of Mission

How should schools be understood as learning communities? Communities are defined by their centers—repositories of values, sentiments, and beliefs that provide the needed cement for bonding people together in a common cause. Community centers operate much like a religion by providing norms that structure what we do, how we do it, and why we do it. They answer such questions as these: What is this school about? What is our image of learners? What makes us unique? How do we work together? How does the school as community fit into the larger school system? How do parents fit into the picture? Why are all these questions worth asking and answering? If schools are viewed as learning communities, such questions are typical and, as such, are honored and contribute to the professional level of a learning school.

Sergiovanni (1992) offers, among others, a case study involving Griffin Elementary School in Los Angeles. Yvonne Davis, the former principal of the school, stated that the transformation of the school occurred gradually. Teachers began to relax and became open to new ideas and new instructional techniques. Mutual respect grew as greater and greater sharing took place. Davis noted that lunchroom talk was dominated by teachers inquiring about each others' classroom activities. Teaching was no longer done in isolation or privacy. Instead, teachers at the same grade level worked together and developed a stronger sense of accountability for instructional outcomes. A teachers' voice was "no longer concerned only for 'my class' or 'my kids.' Instead all efforts and energies joined force to improve the school as a whole" (p. 50).

You will recall that Senge's impression of schools, echoing Ernest Boyer's (1983) study of the high school, was typified by territorial isolation among teachers. In contrast, Sergiovanni's vision of the school as a moral community emphasizes the need of bringing together notions of leadership, professionalism, community, and shared purpose. When there is a shared covenant of values, leadership possesses moral authority and empowers members to act.

The Leader at the Helm

It is tempting to equate the success of an organization with the capabilities and character of the leader at the helm. Individuals with high visibility and charisma are often seen to lead their organizations through rough waters as Lee Iaccoca did when he was CEO of the Chrysler Corporation. However, both Senge and Sergiovanni dispute the perception that one person is capable of meeting the demands of a contemporary, complex organization.

The leader of a complex organization cannot, alone, deal with all the intricacies of an organization and its challenges. The leader must rely on the capabilities of the organization's members. To achieve the desired level of cooperative behavior from organization members, they must have a stake in the shared vision. It is unrealistic to expect them to do otherwise. When Senge refers to the past problems at General Motors, he identifies the workers' lack of involvement in product quality as the missing ingredient. Those involved in the system of production had only an isolated view of their part in the enterprise; they did not see the system as a whole. Therefore, the workers producing the product did not understand the consequences of their actions until sales fell off to their competitors. When applied to schools, it is apparent that all of a school's staff must work in concert toward a shared vision if the students are to be infused with the value of learning.

Moral Validation of the Authority of Vision

Some leaders may prefer that questions about their leadership not be posed. The position they occupy is sufficient warrant, in their view, for what they do. This leader-at-the-helm mentality assumes that others should follow blindly and without thought. Relying on bureaucratic authority in some cases may be the simplest and most direct way to get things done. When practiced in a school, teachers follow higher authority without question or face the consequences. What is missing is a moral justification of such leadership. It may be efficient in the near term and may command conformity, but is it good and right?

Such traditional leadership style may also have negative consequences. Teachers will, very likely, be forced into defensive postures when a principal or supervisor assumes such an authoritarian position. In addition, the adversarial nature of labor-management relations can be reinforced, thus undercutting common purpose in a school. Overall, authoritarian leadership provides no room for vision to be shared.

Isn't there a better way? We seek a justification for leadership that has a moral grounding. The test for effective leadership is whether it elicits support on the basis of common respect for ideas, ideals, and values, not merely one's place in an administrative hierarchy. Similarly, the test for an action is not whether it works efficiently but whether it is right.

Determining what is right is not easy, as we fully recognize. Nevertheless, a good place to begin is to place the highest priority on learning. Thus, such questions as whether leadership is focused on learning in the school community assume greatest importance. The personality of the leader at the helm is no longer a relevant consideration when emphasis is placed on what the learning school accomplishes. Do students learn what is expected to be learned? Authentic assessment will answer that question. If the answer is negative, the task is clearly one of mitigating the shortcoming.

The moral validation of both leadership and followership rests in the duties and obligations derived from the vision that a learning school shares. There can be no avoiding the moral centrality of shared vision.

Motivation

Hackman and Oldham (1976) identified three psychological states believed to be critical in determining whether a person will be motivated at work:

- *Experienced meaningfulness* refers to developing a sense of worth both of work itself and the person doing it.
- *Experienced responsibility* entails persons believing that they are accountable for what they achieve.
- *Knowledge of results* requires that feedback on a regular basis be given so that individuals are able to determine whether the outcomes of their efforts are satisfactory (Hackman, Oldham, Johnson, & Purdy, 1975, cited in Sergiovanni, 1992, p. 60).

It is important that a learning school should be constantly working toward the kind of community where experiences of meaningfulness, responsibility, and knowledge of results are permanent. This entails engaging the talents and skills of all members in the learning organization in problem seeking and problem identification: developing strategies that use available skills in problem solving, and devising mechanisms for consultation about progress. Such behaviors can offset the stultifying defensiveness often found in traditional bureaucratic structures.

Intrinsic Motivation and Flow in Work

What is intrinsic to motivation in one's work is the reward the work itself brings. People can be so totally absorbed by a task that they lose track of time. What they are involved with completely absorbs them. The work is its own reward.

Borrowing from the research of Mihalyi Csikszentmihalyi (1990), Sergiovanni discusses the concept of "flow" in work. Flow refers to those moments when all things come together and one has a feeling of realized accomplishment. Something has been done not because you were told to but because the activity was rewarding in and of itself. In short, you have a sense of command and ownership from beginning to end.

All too seldom are such flow experiences given to educators. Too often, they are following directions from a superordinate authority. Teachers, for example, must follow schedules mandated by someone else and curricula defined by textbooks adopted by someone else. This results in teachers having little or no involvement in developing the purposes of what they do. Consequently, teaching can become routinized to the point where it becomes a thoughtless habit without careful regard for the response of the learners. At the same time, there is minimal motivation and even less reward for the work.

How different it could be if teachers share in the determination of their work and its environment. Clearly, one significant mark of a learning school is such involvement.

Purposing

An important aspect of shared vision in a learning school is the concept of *common purpose*. What is at stake is a connection between what any single individual does and the institution's larger purpose. In this regard, Sergiovanni (1992) quotes Peter Vaill (1984) in defining *purposing* as "that continuous stream of actions by an organization's formal leadership which has the effect of inducing clarity, consensus and commitment regarding the organization's basic purpose" (p. 73). Hence, Sergiovanni notes, "purposing involves both the vision of school leaders and the covenant that the school shares" (p. 73). It will be remembered that vision, in Senge's (1990) formulation, is shared. Apparently, for Sergiovanni (1992) a *covenant* is the vehicle for such sharing: "A covenant provides the added dimension of values and moral authority to make purposing count," and further, "When both the value of vision and the value-added dimension of covenant are present, teachers and students respond with increased motivation and commitment" (p. 73).

The experience of Hank Cotton, principal of Cherry Creek High School in Englewood, Colorado is an example in Sergiovanni's view. Cotton successfully turned around the school's decline in several areas. Most significant for this discussion, he directed his leadership to developing a set of shared values and commitments that bonded the faculty together in a common cause variously referred to as purposing and shared vision. Leadership by such bonding allows for moral authority to become the basis for leadership. What was central in Cotton's leadership was the sharing of values and vision intertwined. The sharing allowed him to sit on the sidelines and let shared values drive leadership. Accordingly, this kind of leadership is based on purposes owned by all in a learning school. Without such sharing, members of a school have no say in their expressed purposes and must give assent to a leader in a subservient manner.

The Culture of Collegiality

We have already noted the isolation of teachers in most schools. Boyer's (1983) commentary on the isolation of public secondary school teachers rings true. Sergiovanni (1992) presents collegiality among teachers and administrators as a reform strategy. Collegiality, in his view, is a professional virtue. He cites Roland Barth (1990), who sees it as the key ingredient in the notion of a school as a community of learners. The more collegiality becomes established in a school, the more natural will connections among people become and the more they will become self-managed. But collegiality in schools is rare. The problem, very largely, seems to occur in a culture of schooling characterized by bureaucratic norms of management that reinforce the isolation and privatism of teachers. Change from such isolationism to a more collegial atmosphere is not accomplished simply by a superordinate (i.e., administrator) mandating behavioral change to a subordinate (i.e., teacher). Administrators, for example, who push for collegiality by altering schedules or ways of work through the introduction of such innovations as team teaching and peer coaching in a school without addressing the overall administrative structure necessary to alter a school's culture may be superimposing a form of collegiality on an unaccepting culture. When this occurs the people who are to be colleagues are, ironically, not involved in the decision to make the change. Such contrived collegiality can be counterproductive. Those not involved in the decision-making process will have no experience of either the meaning or the need for greater collegiality. As Sergiovanni (1992) sums up,

> Collegiality cannot be understood in the abstract. What makes two people colleagues is common membership in a community, commitment to a common cause, shared professional values, and a shared professional heritage. Without this common base, there can be no meaningful collegiality. (p. 91)

Mooney's (1990) analysis of the teacher professionalism project in the Pittsburgh Public School District revealed that conflicting cultures of bureaucratic control and new collegial programs can obstruct implementation. Institutional patterns may remain quite bureaucratic even as reform toward consensual governance is attempted. A conflict of two different organizational paradigms occurs, resulting in a kind of "paradigmatic ambiguity." The question of how teachers and administrators can operate by the rules of one culture some of the time and a different culture at other times must be answered. Clearly, the entire system has to embrace a new culture for collegiality to work. This cultural dimension of school reform underlines the need for shared vision in the system. Reform efforts without integration of systemic elements will fail.

Control: Differentiation and Coordination

Closely related to the cultural issue is the control paradox. Sergiovanni (1992) quotes the Canadian management scholar, Henry Mintzberg (1979):

> Every organized human activity . . . gives rise to two fundamental and opposing requirements: the *division of labor* into various tasks to be performed and the *coordination* of these tasks to accomplish the activity. The structure of an organization can be captured simply as the sum total of ways in which it divides its labor into distinct tasks and then achieves coordination among them. (cited in Sergiovanni, 1992, p. 92)

School leaders, whether they are building principals or area and district superintendents, face such a situation. What is at stake here is finding ways to balance differentiation of tasks with coordination among organizational parts. Sergiovanni regards this as a paradox, but we suggest that this is a common tension open to reconciliation. Collegiality among leaders and followers is one way to bring about such needed reconciliation. Mintzberg (1979) graphically describes a classical leadership model: "They see themselves perched atop metaphorical hierarchies, there to impose the control of 'superior' minds over everyone else, the 'subordinates'" (quoted in Graham, 1995, p. 202). Instead of accepting such a top-down management model, leadership in collegial terms strives to bring together views of both followers and leaders in a shared vision.

Alternatives to Collegiality

There are, however, alternatives to a collegial style of management, some of which relate to collegiality, whereas others are antithetical:

- Direct supervision
- Standardizing the work of teaching
- Standardizing the outcomes of teaching

- Emphasizing professional socialization
- Emphasizing purposing and shared values

Direct supervision, standardized work, and standardized outputs do not rely on collegiality. Each can be enforced by administrative demands or commands. Direct supervision relies on a designated leader giving initial directions and closely supervising ensuing work. While that may be an appropriate management model for easily routinized work, in Sergiovanni's (1992) view it can work for "fast-food restaurants but not for schools" (p. 93).

Similarly, standardized work processes are a form of coordination commensurate with environments where work can easily be predicted. If responsibility, as in teaching, varies according to situation or client, standardization does not pertain. It may work "for Federal Express but not for schools, where work is more complex" (Sergiovanni, 1992, p. 94).

In contrast, standardizing the outcomes of teaching may lead to greater latitude by allowing greater individual freedom in various teaching episodes. Particularly in a day when there is greater sensitivity to multiple intelligences among learners (Gardner, 1988), such freedom can be important. At the same time, emphasis on outcomes, particularly if outcomes are measured in terms of standardized tests, might dictate standardized methods of instruction (e.g., memorization of answers to typical test questions) that are less than adequate for meaning making. This is not a negative criticism of standardized tests so much as a caution about their use. If evaluated outcomes are employed as general indicators for a group or grade level, they may be useful diagnostic tools (formative as opposed to summative evaluation). When they are used as cutoff standards, separating performers from nonperformers, they are open to question.

Despite problems associated with them, direct supervision, standardized work, and standardized outputs remain popular because they reflect typical values of management. Sergiovanni sees greater value and more relevant applicability in collegiality for developing shared vision in a learning school. As such, collegiality involves an emphasis on professional socialization, common purposing, and shared values.

Collegiality and Natural Interdependence

The key to collegiality is natural—that is, not manipulated—interdependence. Once teaching and administration are seen to be mutually interdependent, then leadership can be less intense—indeed, much more informal. Control and coordination evolve naturally as teachers and administrators respond to forces from within. Simplified and more sensitive management systems have a tendency to free people to behave responsibly in complex situations. As collegiality is more broadly experienced, the need for intervention by administrative leadership decreases. Interaction among teachers can relieve administrators of day-to-day, direct, personal leadership, thereby freeing them to establish conditions that encourage collegiality and leadership among teacher peers (Sergiovanni, 1992, p. 98).

Summary: A Vision Ethic for Schools

There are currently many studies and proposals for educational reform. To list them all could result in a giant patchwork of ideas for improvement. What is valuable, however, is a larger view of what kind of organization schools ought to be. Senge's (1990) concept of the learning organization and Sergiovanni's (1992) notion of moral leadership are major contributions to such a larger view. Senge, writing primarily for the American corporation, proposes that institutions and organizations function as integrated organisms that learn how to improve their output. Sergiovanni believes that a moral dimension should exist in the leadership of organizations, particularly schools, which is secured by a covenant of ideas, values, and commitments shared by the members of the organization.

We believe that a synthesis of Senge and Sergiovanni results in the larger picture of the nature of schools that we feel is needed. What evolves from this synthesis is a school that is a dynamic and interactive learning organization. Such an organization takes its character from the shared ideas and values of its members. The authority of such a school is enhanced by a covenant that bolsters its decisions and policies. The shared vision, the sense of group mission, which the school staff possesses, acts as a guiding light in the public arena. For students in such a school, the model of learning is applied to life and work.

Part II of this book builds a rationale for such a learning school. Whether it is called a *virtuous school* (Sergiovanni's term) or a *learning organization* (Senge's term), such a school would have hallmarks of collegiality and shared vision.

Part II

How to Implement Vision-Based Leadership

5

Translating Deep
Beliefs Into Practice

An Integrated Model

In the previous chapters, we dealt with important theoretical matters regarding educational leadership for the learning school. We
emphasized shared vision as the starting point for school reform.
The development of a vision supported by all major stakeholders
prevents school reform from becoming a casualty of intragroup snip-
ing and subversion.

It is necessary to analyze and review deep beliefs about knowledge and learning in order to develop a shared vision. To that end,
we examined several major philosophical and psychological foundations of education. We also surveyed two current theories of organizational leadership (Senge, 1990, and Sergiovanni, 1992) that address
the overarching concerns of school reform relevant to the needs of
the present and the turnover to a new century. These theories highlight the idea of shared vision but with an important added feature—
moral authority. A central element of school reform is determining
what constitutes a good education. These value judgments are a constant concern to stakeholders. We do not prescribe what a good education is in any specific sense. However, we do insist that learning
organizations need to provide a moral rationale for their actions.
Translating deeply held beliefs into practice involves both a theoreti-
cally and morally informed grounding.

In this chapter, we present a model for a learning school. It consists
initially of four integrated elements: shared vision, authentic teaching and learning, supportive school organization, and assessment.
The elements of the model are interdependent and need to be under-

stood holistically and not sequentially. Without one or another of the elements the model is incomplete.

We next explain how to move from theory to practice by presenting ways to implement shared vision in existing schools or charter schools devised by various charter participants. For these, we rely on the research of Fred M. Newmann and his colleagues at the Center on Organization and Restructuring of Schools in Madison, Wisconsin to analyze authenticity in the teaching-learning-assessment relation.

The basis of our position is this:

- Without a leading vision shared by stakeholders there can be no sense of educational outcomes instrumental to students' meaning making.
- The vision needs to include deep beliefs about teaching and learning.
- Honest and thorough assessment will not occur without a school organization supportive of envisioned outcomes.
- Without assessment there is no way to determine what learning has been achieved.

When integrated, these elements—shared vision, authentic teaching and learning, supportive organization, and assessment—provide an initial definition of the learning school. In this chapter and the next, we elaborate the model.

Conceptual Framework

The rationale for an integrated model for the learning school is based on the concept that a school should be a community for learning. While that may seem on the surface to be a truism, to many people schools represent a variety of unrelated goals and objectives. These can include employment for geographic constituents, custodial care for parents, job training for students, and meaning making among students and teachers. Such variety in goals represents a challenge to establish priorities. Because of this, an educator's vision needs to highlight meaning making as a prime goal. If a school or a school district does not give status to meaning making, none of the other services it may provide, such as job training, custodial care, or employment of professionals, has value.

Contrary to standard administrative practice, where leadership resides in an administrator at the apex of a hierarchy, the vision we have described requires participation by stakeholders at all levels. When such shared vision is focused on meaning making, administrative support concentrates on what is required to provide such outcomes. The issue then is not who leads but what lead everyone follows.

Such a vision obviously requires a shift from leadership based on a top-down bureaucratic system to a more open system of shared leadership. An open system of leadership is not an invitation to vagueness or chaos. It is not an organizational system without controls or boundaries. The controls and boundaries of the system are defined by the people participating in them. To those who might charge that such openness allows the school to be administrated by the inmates, we point out that learning as meaning making is largely a matter of what makes sense to learners. Do learners, therefore, have complete charge over what they should learn? Of course not. If the notion of learners includes teachers and administrators and parents and other community members as well as students, then instructional design is a product of shared vision. In this connection, the interpretation of John Dewey's educational philosophy by Nel Noddings (1984) is pertinent:

> The principle of the leading out of experience does not imply letting the child learn what he pleases; it suggests that, inescapably, the child will learn what he pleases. That means that the educator must arrange the effective world so that the child will be challenged to master significant tasks in significant situations. The initial judgment of significance is the teacher's task. (p. 63)

Four Elements for School Restructuring: An Integrated Model

Vision in education should focus on learning processes and outcomes (Figure 5.1). Accordingly, vision and learning processes and

Vision ⟷ Learning Processes and Outcomes
(Authentic Instruction
Authentic Assessment
Authentic Student Work)

Figure 5.1.

outcomes define each other and are mutually interdependent. Learning processes and outcomes require a nexus of the teaching-learning interchange involving, in our view, authentic pedagogy. For the purposes of this illustration, we use Newmann's concept of authentic pedagogy (including instruction, assessment, and student work; Newmann & Associates, 1996, p. 11) to represent our value position. As the diagrams of the integrated model are developed progressively, we will substitute authentic instruction, authentic student work, and authentic assessment for learning processes and outcomes. Authentic pedagogy encompasses the constructivist perspective of meaning making that is central to our vision. Consequently, the diagram is developed further (Figure 5.2).

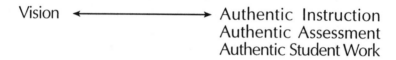

Figure 5.2.

At the same time, such learning processes and outcomes require a supportive organizational system—the learning organization. It has already been noted that vision is to be shared among major stakeholders. Accordingly, the organization of a learning school needs to account for the reciprocity of both vision and outcomes (Figure 5.3).

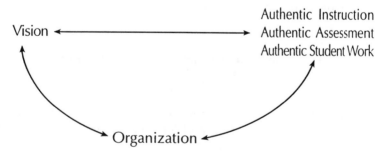

Figure 5.3.

Assessment, as part of the integrated model, refers to those evaluative activities used by the stakeholders in the learning school to gather information to improve the effectiveness of the organization. Assessment influences learning processes and outcomes as members of the organization form a professional community to examine the impact of pedagogy on student learning. Teachers and principals in the learning school will inquire about the assessment of student learning and reflect on how they can improve the quality of student work. In this sense, assessment serves a vital function in the learning school (Figure 5.4).

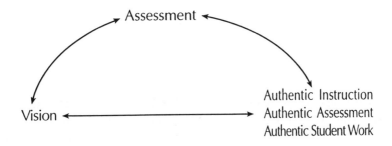

Figure 5.4.

At the same time, assessment influences the vision statement of the learning school. The members of the learning community continually examine the current state of the school in relation to the vision. The vision for the learning school will have to be modified based on the experiences of implementation. Thus, assessing the efficacy of the vision statement through the analysis of multiple sources of data provides the evidentiary base for vision modification. As previously stated, assessment serves a vital function in helping the learning school to evaluate the effectiveness of its support structure in achieving the vision and the conditions for learning processes and outcomes.

The integrated model in diagrammatic form (Figure 5.5) illustrates the interdependence of all four elements. Outcomes are defined by vision. Assessment evaluates the degree to which outcomes are achieved. Organization facilitates feedback among the other variables:

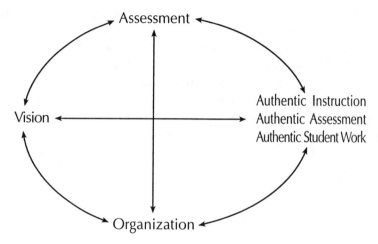

Figure 5.5.

vision, outcome, and assessment. Without the feedback facilitated by organizational arrangements, the model can become frozen in time and circumstance and therefore unable to relate to changing conditions. In other words, vision and learning outcomes are basic starting points in the reform process. Organization and assessment facilitate school practice. All four elements are interdependent. Restructured educational practice is incomplete if one of the elements is missing. A vision of reformed educational outcomes is dependent on an organization that allows for both a new sense of what a learning school is to achieve and the assessment necessary to evaluate its progress.

Authenticity

What constitutes authenticity in regard to these matters is not only a fair question but also a natural one. In this respect, we have found the work of the Wisconsin Center on Organization and Restructuring of Schools to be a pathfinder. Authentic teaching and learning need to be geared to such instrumental skills as construction of knowledge, disciplined inquiry, and value beyond schooling (Newmann & Wehlage, 1995). We have previously referred to these skills as meaning making, where besides making meaning, the meanings made are geared to some further accomplishment.

As Newmann and colleagues point out, constructing knowledge is a complex task dependent on such instrumental skills as organizing, synthesizing, interpreting, explaining, and evaluating information. A learner does not accomplish this easily. People depend on the prior knowledge of others. People need to be guided through practice in discussion and analytic writing to sort out what they believe and know and value. Cognitive capacity develops through stages, as Piaget's research on child development reveals. To expect, for example, that a child can learn subtle similarities and differences in the volume of differently shaped containers is not realistic at very early developmental stages. At the same time, a child need not learn things that must be unlearned later. As Jerome Bruner (1993) and others have noted, humans can learn anything in some correct form at any developmental stage. Unlike a curriculum that relies excessively or even wholly on mimicry or memorization, an emphasis on knowledge construction requires increasing degrees of the analytic and synthetic skills instrumental to meaning making.

Second, such skills require disciplined inquiry. Typically, inquiry in any topical area recounts prior knowledge and then proceeds to a careful definition of the problem under review. Students in a learning school need to move beyond a simple recounting of previous knowledge. They need to understand the issues associated with a problem in any given curriculum area and consider alternatives in meeting problems. Students must also provide a rationale for the conclusions they reach. We agree "that all students are capable of engaging in these forms of cognitive work when the work is adapted to students' levels of development" (Newmann & Wehlage, 1995, p. 9).

Although Newmann and his colleagues did not examine in depth the value of knowledge beyond schooling, we can hypothesize its importance. What one learns in school is never an end in itself. Or if it is, its utility is limited. Worthwhile achievements go beyond simply proving one's ability to someone else. If the skill exhibited is writing, its purpose is not merely to display the skill but to communicate something in writing to others. As Newmann and Wehlage (1995) state, "Authenticity calls for student accomplishments ... beyond simply showing the teacher, the parent, a college, or an employer that the student has mastered the requirements of schooling" (p. 11). In this day of the information explosion, it is obvious that what one learns in school must have utility beyond schooling. Without critical thinking skills that enable persons to make evaluations about information, they are simply crippled for life and work in the "information age."

Accordingly, when we speak of outcomes in terms of authentic instruction, authentic student work, and authentic achievement, we mean having brought learners to a point of readiness for a productive and satisfying adult life. The adult world does not consist of simple true-false or multiple-choice tests. Students need to be enabled to think for themselves and make the meaningful choices that will be required of them for the rest of their lives.

Three Standards for Authentic
Teaching and Learning

The Center on Organization and Restructuring of Schools (CORS) has developed standards for authentic pedagogy and student performance. Three overarching standards are central for consideration here: construction of knowledge, disciplined inquiry, and value beyond schooling (Newmann & Wehlage, 1995, p. 10).

A learning school needs to promote thoughtful discussion among stakeholders of these standards to tailor them to specific situations. It also bears repeating that the CORS standards have only been developed for mathematics and social studies. However, there is no reason why they cannot be adapted to apply to other curriculum areas.

Construction of knowledge obviously moves beyond the sheer recitation of data. The CORS standards point to such matters as the ability to organize content, synthesizing, interpreting, hypothesizing, describing patterns, making comparisons and contrasts, applying information in new contexts, and considering, especially in such areas as social studies and literature, alternative points of view. Earlier, we noted that knowledge is, in some sense, socially constructed, which suggests that teachers need to be aware of the social forces influencing themselves and others in the process of making meaning of what is learned.

Disciplined inquiry involves demonstrating an understanding of central concepts as well as making connections among such concepts and how they influence understanding. Emphasis is placed on developing systematic thought, distinguishing between fact and opinion (especially in social studies), and understanding applications to life situations. Our highlighting of meaning making is dependent on those skills that prepare learners to increasingly embark on disciplined inquiry on their own.

The third CORS standard, *value beyond schooling*, is admittedly presented in relatively unfinished form. Nevertheless, learning as making meaning is not a short-term pursuit but an ongoing activity. For example, we learn to read not as an end in itself but as an instrument for a great deal of other learning. The same is true for other academic disciplines. As a standard, value beyond school calls for making *"connections to the world beyond the classroom"* (Newmann & Wehlage, 1995, p. 18). Although this standard may not be open to quick or easy assessment, still it represents a value central to authentic teaching and learning. Every student, as well as every teacher, needs to ask "So what?" at the end of every lesson, every reading assignment, and every writing project.

Authentic Assessment

A critical element in the integrated model is assessment. Currently, there are some who would create national standards for learning outcomes. We do not disapprove of such national standards, but we do caution against their use as a quick or sufficient fix. National standards can play a useful role in defining base points in learning in any academic area. Individual schools or individual school districts should not mechanically translate such standards into instructional practice and thereby develop means for assessing learning outcomes. The process of assessment is not that simple. Interrelationship between assessment and instruction is needed. It requires extensive analysis and discussion among teachers about the content and quality of educational outcomes.

Presently, there is only partial agreement among experts in various curriculum fields about standards. But learning schools do not need to wait for broad consensus on standards in all academic disciplines to assess what is learned. As learning communities, such schools can discuss and evaluate the learning occurring within their walls. The CORS standards, developed only in areas of social studies and mathematics, can usefully be applied as a research and discussion tool that groups of teachers can employ in other curriculum areas to assess both teaching and learning. Typical questions to be raised in this regard include the following: Are higher-order thinking skills being promoted in these areas? Does student learning demonstrate meaning making beyond the identification of dates and events or correct answers? Has the structure of such disciplines been learned in a way that enables students to learn more on their own?

More specifically, authentic assessment can follow the CORS standards for authentic teaching and learning. As Newmann, Secada, and Wehlage (1995) have noted, "Authentic academic accomplishment, instruction and assessment must aim toward tasks that demand construction of knowledge through disciplined inquiry and that result in discourse, products, and performance that have value or meaning beyond success in school" (p. 14). Earlier, three such standards for teaching and learning (construction of knowledge, disciplined inquiry, and value beyond schooling) were enumerated. Here, we analyze them in terms of their application to assessment.

The construction of knowledge can be assessed in terms of two characteristics: the organization of knowledge and the consideration of alternatives. Here, students' work would be assessed in terms of their demonstrating organization, synthesizing (i.e., putting together relevant pieces of information), and interpreting, explaining, or evaluating how the information chosen addresses some problem, issue, or concept. Whether such organizing activity is performed in quantitative or qualitative activities, the factors to be assessed are similar. Newmann et al. (1995) provide two examples: one from mathematics and the other from social studies. In the first case, students were given a problem of providing the measurements of a bookcase to hold an object (or objects) of specific size. To accomplish this task, the students had to organize quantitative information precisely so that the finished bookcase would consist of dimensions that were neither too small nor too large for the object in question. The social studies example dealt with a question about immigration policy and required students to select relevant information about past and present practice and explain how such information addresses current and widely debated issues about immigration (Newmann et al., 1995, pp. 15-16). In each case, authentic assessment focuses on the way in which information is organized.

At the same time, assessing knowledge construction requires students to evaluate and select data from among alternatives. In this regard, Newmann et al. provide a mathematics illustration that required students to evaluate a problem involving the relation of shapes of objects to volume. The problem entailed an emphasis on evaluation of alternative sets of information if volume and shape are correctly related. In the social studies example, students were called upon to construct an argument to support a particular social policy (e.g., U.S. involvement in Vietnam).

Assessing disciplined inquiry can involve the evaluation of content and process and the ability to convey conclusions in written communication. In this case, students in mathematics were given the task of using differently shaped tiles to decorate a classroom. There was no single correct answer. Instead, students, after arranging the tiles, had to provide a written explanation of what surfaces the tiles would and would not cover. In the social studies example, students were directed to write a "persuasive essay" on an issue related to a presidential election. Again, there was no correct answer. Evaluation was based on students' having developed an argument from history and current events which showed the importance of such matters for citizens voting in the democratic process (Newmann & Wehlage, 1993).

What can be most lasting for learning is its value beyond schooling. Authentic assessment needs to be mindful of how learning relates to problems in life that are connected to the student's world and how well learning relates to an audience beyond the school and its classrooms. Ultimately for the student as a lifelong learner, what is important is not merely what is accomplished in relation to a classroom objective but how well learning is connected to the world beyond the classroom. In this regard, what is learned needs to be assessed in terms of whether and how adequately it addresses some audience beyond the school. Practical learning can be assessed in terms of real-life situations. For example, in mathematics the design of packaging to hold specified amounts of some product constitutes a real-life problem. In social studies, the analysis of an actual social issue, such as a problem in race relations, is instrumental to the application of learning with consequences beyond schooling.

Newmann and Wehlage (1995, p. 15) elaborate the three initial standards for authentic teaching and learning to seven standards for authentic assessment:

- Construction of Knowledge
  1. Organization of information
  2. Consideration of alternatives

- Disciplined Inquiry
  3. Disciplinary content
  4. Disciplinary process
  5. Elaborated written communication
- Value Beyond Schooling
  6. Problem connected to the world
  7. Audience beyond schooling

We are suggesting that assessment of both teaching and learning needs to account for meaning making. If facts for a student do not enable and excite further learning, then something in teaching has failed. This does not mean that one teacher or another is a failure. It does mean that in terms of outcomes some learning has not occurred. To ensure greater success, more attention needs to be given to what was taught and how it was taught.

It is important to note that Newmann and Wehlage (1995) have entered a caveat about all of these standards: "One would not expect all activities to meet all . . . standards all the time" (p. 11). Drill and practice, memorization, and simple information retrieval activities do not sufficiently meet standards for authenticity in teaching and learning. Yet such activities are necessary to develop the rudimentary skills that facilitate meaning making. Still, the standards provide useful ways to assess learning and evaluate a learning school.

Developing a Professional Community

Essential for the kind of learning school suggested by the integrated model is a professional community (see Chapters 6 and 9), which is a place where interaction among school professionals is nurtured and focused on learning outcomes for students and the organization. The description of the teacher isolated within a classroom in teaching-learning tasks is all too familiar. In contrast, a professional community highlights interchange among teachers and between teachers and administrators and genuine conversation with other stakeholders (e.g., parents, other community members). Of course, facilitating such interaction calls for change in schools' organizational structure. Even more, it requires a change in school culture.

Among the characteristics of a professional community are reflective dialogue, greater interaction among teacher colleagues or what may be called *deprivatization* of instructional practice (Louis, Marks, & Kruse, 1994), collective focus on student learning, collaboration among educational professionals, and shared values and norms. In this section, we describe these features as they contribute to the development of the learning school. In the next chapter, they are analyzed in terms of their contribution to shared governance.

Reflective dialogue reflects on practice and brings to the fore what has been done in teaching and learning. It opens the way for critical analysis by observers and makes available a spectrum of ideas about what one intends to accomplish in teaching episodes. As such, it should lead to collaboration among teachers intent on improving instruction. But it requires openness to formative evaluation among collaborators.

Deprivatization of instructional practice entails the development of relationships among teachers where they "can share and trade-off the roles of mentor, advisor, or specialist when aiding and assisting peers" (Louis et al., 1994, p. 3). We have already noted that teachers, especially in isolation from other professionals (Boyer, 1983, pp. 158, 160, 171; Cuban, 1984, pp. 252-253), are not enabled to learn from others and benefit from the analysis and feedback of what they customarily do when they are teaching. If reflective dialogue among teachers is to occur, the culture of teacher isolation needs to be changed.

Collective focus on student learning may seem to be obvious, but the question of focus is crucial. A learning school is characterized by a professional community intent on producing student learning outcomes. Priority is placed on activities whose basic purpose is not simple enjoyment but student growth. As such, a professional community engaged in reflective dialogue spends its time discussing and analyzing curriculum and instructional strategies that promote meaning making and the development of students as self-starting learners.

Collaboration starts when teachers break out of isolation and can call upon the expertise of others within the professional community. No professionals are complete in themselves and beyond further improvement and development. Accordingly, professional collaborators enable each other through mutual analysis to deal with the complex needs of individual learners and build a community of support to sustain each other in their daily tasks.

Shared norms and values are established when various professionals—teachers, supervisors, counselors, administrators—are brought together to identify what they have in common. By establishing shared norms and values for a learning school, these professionals will develop the kind of moral authority that Sergiovanni (1992) highlights.

The development of professional communities requires several structural attributes of a learning school: time to meet and discuss, establishment of class size, teacher empowerment, and school autonomy (Louis et al., 1994).

Time to meet and discuss is necessary. Research on school and teacher effectiveness indicates that time set aside for teacher consultation is needed. Typically, teachers move from class to class and assignment to assignment without opportunities for professional collaboration. Group need should determine appropriate teaching strategies. In any case, scheduled time for teacher interaction is a requisite for collaboration.

Class size, according to research, is equivocal. Nevertheless, some studies have shown that class size needs to be kept at a minimum (Altenbaugh, Engel, & Martin, 1995; Bennett & LeCompte, 1990; Pittman & Haughwout, 1987) to gain positive learning outcomes. One teacher in a classroom can effectively relate to only a limited number of students. Although there is no magic number in regard to class size, it stands to reason that as class size is increased a teacher's ability to relate and respond to students is stretched.

Teacher empowerment and *school autonomy* are necessary for teachers to feel that they can act as they see fit in individual classroom settings. This empowerment coincides with shared governance for a learning school. At the same time, individual schools within a larger system should have sufficient autonomy to relate to the needs of the variety of students in their domain. Of course, school systems, as individual schools, should have developed common, overarching goals and objectives. Within a shared vision, individual circumstances will require individual initiatives and responses on the part of teachers and school leaders. We do not know of one best way of teaching or administrating a school, but with reflective dialogue, collaboration, and shared norms and values, teachers can be empowered to work on their own. Similarly, individual schools can best decide, through site-based management and school-based decision making, the appropriate means for implementing districtwide policy. This is not to suggest complete autonomy for individual schools and teachers. It is to recommend autonomy for schools within agreed-on guidelines and policies of the larger district and latitude for teachers to act responsively and responsibly to students in their care.

Requisites for the development of a professional community culture are human and social resources. They include an openness to innovation, trust and respect among major stakeholders, a cognitive skill base, and supportive leadership.

Openness to innovation requires that professionals in a learning school be willing to take risks, to experiment, and to find ways to improve student performance. One expects that the kind of reflective dialogue among teachers as described above will include analysis of new and revised approaches to pedagogy. The culture of the entire school needs to provide clear support of those who take the initiative in implementing innovations. Not all innovations will have positive outcomes, but if they are never tried, reflective dialogue has no way of assessing the good and the bad.

Trust and respect, both from internal and external stakeholders, characterize a professional community. As Louis et al. (1994) note, "Respect refers to the honoring of the expertise of others, while trust refers more to the quality of interpersonal relations" (p. 7). Interpersonal relations are the product of reflective dialogue and collaboration. Trust and respect might seem to pertain primarily to relations among teachers. We extend the definition to refer to other stakeholders as well, such as school administrators, parents, and other members of the larger community surrounding the school. To be sure, teachers in public schools are viewed as public servants, but we emphasize their service, not their servitude. If teachers' attention is centered on meaning making and the learning outcomes of students, they should command respect and trust. All too often, critics of education have faulted teachers as if they were the sole culprits in school performance. Yet any thoughtful analysis of school problems will recognize the role and responsibility of other parties for a learning school. Are school administrators instrumental in creating a positive school climate? Are parents supportive of their children's development? If teachers have a sufficient cognitive and skill base, then they should be given respect and trust.

A cognitive skill base is an obvious requirement for teachers in a learning school. Teachers need to be secure in their grasp of the knowledge base and the skills for meaning making in their field. Of course, such knowledge and skill is not formed once and for all time. Through continuing educational experiences teachers can and should be kept up-to-date in their respective fields. A learning school prizes such teacher development.

Supportive leadership is critical for the openness, the trust and re- spect, and the development of teachers' cognitive and skill bases to become manifest in a learning school. Research indicates that these matters are requisites in restructured schools (Louis et al., 1994). Re- wards for innovative initiatives are instrumental in a learning school. As reported by Louis et al. (1994), "Leaders . . . who are able to identify and reward actions that further the vision and mission of the school are crucial for organizational innovation" (p. 8).

Summary

Our concern in this chapter has been to provide a basis for trans- lating deep beliefs into practice. Our conceptual framework includes the priority of shared vision and the need for open and facilitating administrative systems.

The integrated model was presented as a guide to practice for the learning school. The model highlights four elements: vision, authentic teaching and learning, school organization, and assess- ment. Because authenticity in teaching, learning, and assessment is central to the model, an accompanying analysis of authenticity was developed. It was described in terms of a demonstrated ability to construct knowledge from information, which, in turn, requires dis- ciplined inquiry as instrumental to meaning making. Resultant meanings made were seen as the basis for further accomplishment. As such, learning how to learn is not an empty slogan but the rigor- ous use of knowledge and skill to make sense of what humans con- front in life.

The integrated model also needs to include means for assess- ment. In this connection, three standards for assessing teaching and learning developed by the CORS were presented. Closely following the marks of authenticity, the standards are construction of knowl- edge, disciplined inquiry, and value beyond schooling, all three of which are instrumental to meaning making. To gain specificity, the three teaching and learning standards were elaborated to seven elements for the purpose of assessing what teaching has accomplished and what learning has occurred.

Instrumental for the realization of the integrated model for the learning school is the concomitant development of a professional community within the school. Such a community is characterized by reflective dialogue and greater interaction (deprivatization) among teachers for the purpose of collective focusing on student development. Overall, such a professional community is grounded in collaboration with shared norms and values.

What lies ahead as we look further in implementing vision-based leadership? One paramount challenge is achieving shared governance in learning communities. Such shared governance is an important cornerstone in school reform.

6

Achieving Shared Governance of the Learning Community

The Cornerstone of the Learning School

In the preceding chapter, we presented an integrated model for vision-based educational leadership. We also suggested that the development of a professional community was instrumental for its realization. As described, a professional community has five features: (a) reflective dialogue, (b) interaction among teacher colleagues (deprivatization), (c) collective focus on student learning, (d) collaboration among education professionals, and (e) shared values and norms.

In turn, such features suggested four structural needs in the operations of a school: (a) time during the workweek to meet and discuss, (b) establishment of class sizes, (c) empowerment of teachers, and (d) school autonomy.

At the same time, such school governance requires, in our estimation, the following: faculty and administration open to innovation; trust and respect among colleagues; a cognitive skill base for all professionals; and leadership supportive of all the above requisites, structural needs and features of a professional community, and shared decision making.

In short, to make a learning school operational, *shared governance* is needed. In this chapter, we provide a process for developing shared governance. Such a process could be developed for a single school as the examples in Chapter 7 will indicate. Nevertheless, this should not preclude instituting the process in an entire school district.

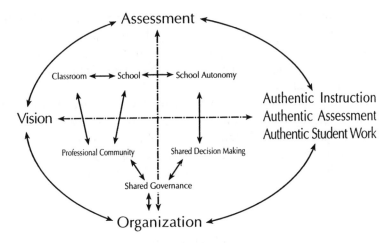

Figure 6.1.

Traditionally, schools have been governed on the basis of a hierarchical decision making model not unlike a factory or the military with prescribed roles for personnel in a command structure with highest authority at the apex. Such top-down management when practiced in a school assumes that teachers are subservient to the principal who alone makes all decisions. Relationships between a principal and teachers can hardly be called collaborative in such situations because of the absence of reciprocity in decision making and management.

Because of the emphasis here on shared governance, we have augmented the integrated model to include additional features of a professional community (see Figure 6.1)

Shared Governance

In general, shared governance can refer to a broad range of matters from instructional policies and practices to decisions related to budget and personnel. What is important is that the people affected by such policies (e.g., teachers) be involved in the decision-making process, especially in regard to issues associated with instruction and student learning.

On a day-by-day basis, it is teachers who are most involved with instruction and student learning. Any policies or procedural decisions will have the greatest impact on them. If such decisions exclude teacher involvement, governance is not shared and consensual support is questionable.

Within school systems or districts, the law typically places final authority in a board of school directors. Nevertheless, there is no reason why those most affected at the level of an individual school should be excluded from the decision process. If governance of a school is shared, then input in decisions is an important part of the process.

School Autonomy

We recognize that public schools typically are grouped in terms of a system or school district. The isolated one-room schoolhouse is a thing of the past. It is our contention that individual schools within a school district need some degree of autonomy in order to exercise shared governance. This is especially true in the current environment where one school can differ significantly from others. Autonomy is a necessary instrument for reform.

Without question, school districtwide policies are the responsibility of school directors in collaboration with the superintendent. At the building level, however, initiative for budget development, implementation, and monitoring are best handled through shared decision making between principal and teachers. Similarly, personnel recruitment, selection, induction, and evaluation are most efficiently and effectively dealt with by the individual school. Although administrative policies are typically developed for a school system by a district board of education, the fine tuning and application of policy necessarily occurs at the building level based on ongoing shared decision making. For example, school scheduling and decisions related to the administration of district discipline policies are best supported when left to shared decisions at the level of individual schools.

We emphasize, however, that school autonomy is not a blank check. Autonomous schools should not be independent of accountability at the district level. Still, they need day-to-day freedom to function according to their best efforts. Accordingly, a learning school is an autonomous school accountable to its immediate constituency (i.e., community, parents, students) and in the long term the larger district (i.e., school directors, superintendent). We emphasize that school autonomy should succeed within a context of teachers and principals being accountable to the community, parents, and school district.

Shared Decision Making

We have emphasized the importance of shared decision making as a central element of shared governance. The issue here is a matter of the extent of shared decision making. We envision a decision-making continuum. This includes some matters (e.g., district-mandated policies and procedures) that the principal enacts. Also, it relates to matters where faculty input is central (e.g., scheduling, instruction).

Developing a professional community where all parties share responsibility is of primary importance. In some matters, the principal is the decision maker (e.g., assigning teachers to playground supervision). In other matters, decisions include faculty input (e.g., deciding on the instructional schedule to achieve maximum flexibility for teachers). In all cases, the principal is not merely a paper-pushing administrator but an instructional leader overseeing budgetary, personnel, and instructional matters. As such, the principal as instructional leader engages all relevant parties in decision making. Even in cases where the principal as instructional leader originates or is the sole decision maker, it is incumbent that such administrative decisions be based on consensus.

The goal of such shared decision making is to develop consensus over instruction and student learning. Earlier, we associated knowledge and learning with meaning making. The learning school is a meaning-making school. Accordingly, the vision of the school as a meaning-making instrument is central. To ensure that such a vision is achieved, another ingredient is necessary—the school as a professional community.

The Professional Community

Karen Seashore Louis and Sharon D. Kruse, whose research was central to our description of the school as a professional community in Chapter 5, have analyzed five cases of school restructuring to determine the presence or absence of professional community. Their analysis is based on the five features previously cited—reflective dialogue, deprivatization or interaction among teacher colleagues, collective focus on student learning, collaboration among education professionals, and shared values and norms.

The development of a professional community is a complex process. The five cases analyzed by Louis and Kruse (1995) reveal degrees of accomplishment they typify as achievement by four types of community: mature, developing, fragmented, and static. Such degree differences indicate steps in developing a professional community. The cases provide evidence of success and failure, both of which are instructive for the development of shared governance, shared decision making, and a learning, professional community.

The example cited by Louis and Kruse of a *mature community* is a high school in a large metropolitan center. Describing the essence of the professional community, they note, "Just as inquiry into learning is the school's instructional theme, inquiry into teaching is the faculty's professional theme" (p. 189). The school's focus seems deceptively simple and centers on the interrelated themes of teaching and learning. We state that this focus is deceptively simple because its attainment can be difficult. Of course, a school is a place where learning occurs. But what if it is not? Of course, teachers are to teach. But what if that teaching is not successful? This mature professional community is constantly solving such questions, analyzing their circumstance, and devising ways to mitigate shortcomings.

It is apparent that such a community is mature in that it fosters collaboration among teachers to assess the learning progress of its students. Faculty meetings are not dominated by administrative trivia but are opportunities to reflect on instructional and curricular issues (Louis & Kruse, 1995, p. 189). There is a constant conversation about the conduct of teaching and learning.

To facilitate such rapport, the school schedule allows time for teacher interaction. The physical space is arranged such that faculty offices are in close proximity. As a consequence, teaching is not conducted in privacy, learning is constantly monitored, and the governance of the school is effectively shared.

Not all the cases surveyed by Louis and Kruse are as successful. A second type of school they analyzed has similar features in common with the first, but not as consistent and pervasive. As such, the school is typified as a *developing community*. That is, it has not fully realized its potential but is on the way. What is missing in this case is faculty unity—a faculty speaking with one voice with shared norms and values. Unanimity among the members of any faculty can be difficult to achieve; thus we would not judge any developing professional community negatively except to note the missing element and the need to attain greater unity.

What is positive about this case is the school's focus on professional development. Without question, the focus is on successful student achievement. Instead of being preoccupied by small talk, teachers converse about student learning outcomes. Such concentration is further reinforced by a series of brown-bag lunches featuring university faculty and teachers from the school. These lunches center on instruction, including both what is currently practiced and new innovations in the field.

In turn, time is set aside for teachers to meet and discuss common problems and issues. The focus of meetings, formal and informal, is on what will benefit student learning and how to put it in place. Overall, the school's administration allows for time and space during the school day and week to engage in collaborative discussion.

However, Louis and Kruse (1995) note that "the faculty is still striving to speak in a common voice, with a commonly held set of convictions about students and instruction" (p. 191). Like many schools restructuring and reshaping their educational mission, this is a school in the process of becoming. Unlike the mature professional community cited previously, more and better communication is needed. Still, there is obvious sharing in the main mission of the school. Louis and Kruse note that the school's principal has remained in the background during this development. It is crucial, however, that the principal continue to support the development of this professional community and facilitate the shared decision making necessary for its coming to maturity.

In their studies, Louis and Kruse observed a third type of school that they refer to as a *fragmented community*. Here, unity among faculty is, at best, partial. As a consequence, tension among faculty groupings results in what can best be described as an apathetic group versus an involved group, as well as competition among subgroups.

In one of two cases in this category, the principal withdrew support of teacher-initiated innovations. Thus, divided along the lines of principal and teachers, the prospects for unity in the professional community are significantly undercut. In the other case, although formed as an innovative high-tech school with pockets of expertise in the faculty, all the teachers do not come together in shared activities and values. Some teachers do meet and discuss curricular and pedagogical issues, but these meetings occur outside school time. Thus, some teachers collaborate, and others are very much isolated. As a result, fragmentation continues.

A fourth type discerned in the Louis and Kruse (1995) case studies is the *static community*. In this environment, no one seems able to take the first steps toward restructuring. This is unfortunate because the school has been redesigned to offer a "life experience curriculum." Despite this intention, the faculty lacks skills for "experiential learning." To further compound problems, the school's program is conducted in three geographically dispersed centers, and no time is set aside for collaboration among teachers across the three centers. Outside consultants brought in to assist have failed to provide helpful ideas that the faculty can use to develop a sense of direction. The result is stagnation. As Louis and Kruse conclude, "It (the school, the faculty) wants to change, yet cannot quite find its way; thus, it finds itself stuck and unable to remedy its problems" (p. 194).

We have presented varying degrees of a professional community. One can benefit from the model of mature community by taking account of the five features of professional community, accommodating the four structural needs, and developing four characteristics of behavior (a faculty and administration open to innovation, trust and respect among colleagues, a cognitive skill base for all professionals, and leadership supportive of such features). Of course, that is not easy, but if there is a vision of a professional community centered on teaching and learning for meaning making, then efforts to reform the school experience are worth it.

Ingredients for Developing a
Professional Community

Along with shared governance, several structural elements are necessary for a learning school. We refer to them as ingredients for developing a professional community.

Scheduling time for teachers to meet and discuss is of paramount importance. One of the characteristics of a professional community is collaboration among teachers. It cannot happen on a hit-or-miss basis. The previously cited example of a fragmented community illustrates both the absence of clear time for all teachers to meet and discuss and the concomitant lack of faculty unity. Such teacher discussion time should not be occupied by trivia but, instead, be focused on authentic teaching, learning, and assessment.

At the same time, there is a need for teachers' lives to be lived in proximity. In the case of one static community, teachers are dispersed among three separate geographic centers. Despite an innovative theme driving curriculum and instruction, there is no opportunity for teachers to meet and discuss common concerns. The lack of proximity disallows the kind of interaction and sharing needed in a professional community.

In addition, the Louis and Kruse (1995) research shows the need for interdependent teaching roles and communication structures. For example, teachers from compatible curriculum areas can and should engage in common planning and, where appropriate, develop strategies for team teaching. It is also possible to cut through busy day-to-day schedules by establishing regular meeting times or by using e-mail. For communication to occur, it needs to be intentional, part of the fabric of the school day.

Finally, an essential ingredient in developing professional community is teacher empowerment through school autonomy. Louis and Kruse stress what they call deprivatization. As discussed earlier, one of the problematic features of typical schooling is teachers acting independently of each other (Boyer, 1983; Cuban, 1984; Goodlad, 1984; O'Neil, 1995). That is, teachers' classrooms have become private places where personnel hide from observation and lose the benefits of colleagues' formative feedback. To develop a professional community, such circumstances need to be turned around. A major step in this direction is to allow school autonomy so that teachers can work together to share responsibility for the effective operation of the learning community. In this regard, we are not advocating autonomy for its own sake. The autonomy we have in mind is instrumental in shared decision making and greater accountability among all teachers at the building level.

Steps for Developing a
Professional Community

We have stressed the central importance of shared governance as one element in developing a professional community. Then where is the focus and energy of leadership to be exercised? A thoughtful response (Louis & Kruse, 1995) is that *leadership is from the center*. That is, leadership best comes not from an administrative hierarchy above nor from scattered criticism below. Instead, the center represents the point where affected parties meet to engage in shared decision making. Formal titles (e.g., principal, lead teacher) notwithstanding, what is accomplished in leadership roles, whether formally recognized or informally realized, is of utmost importance. Therefore, whether leadership emanates from the principal's office or from teachers' innovative ideas, the question is whether such initiatives are capable of developing a following. By engaging teachers in shared or consensual decision making the issues relating to governance of a learning school are addressed.

In all such efforts, careful support of teachers is necessary. Some teachers will lead, and others with prudent support will follow. The issue is creating a climate where leadership can emerge and express itself in a process of making shared decisions. Suppose that a criterion for assessment of administrative leadership was the development of teacher leaders. Wouldn't that transform both administrators' and teachers' behaviors? We think so.

Leading from the center means not taking the least daring course of action but, rather, making the greatest possible difference in school development. A learning school is open to taking risks for reforming the educational experience of its primary clients—its students. The old aphorism of nothing ventured, nothing gained still applies.

Throughout, we have stressed leadership informed by vision. Keeping that vision first and foremost is essential. As articulated here, the vision includes authentic teaching and learning in applying knowledge and learning for meaning making. To achieve such vision, all stakeholders need to be involved in sharing decisions that govern a learning school.

So What About Teacher Unions?

Kerchner and Koppich (1993) have conducted research in school districts to determine how teacher unions can contribute to the reform process. What they have discovered is a trend in negotiated contract settlements for agreements beyond traditional wages and hours matters. They refer to such agreements as "Educational Policy Trust Agreements" (hereafter "trust agreements"). In various ways, teacher union contracts have been extended to include educational policy concerns.

The upshot of this trend is, Kerchner and Koppich believe, a new form of unionism, or what they call a professional union. During collective bargaining, issues about professional conduct, professional development, and school policy can readily arise. They may have little to do with wages and hours. More nearly they relate to how education is to proceed and the status of professionals in handling such matters. As such, there are concerns about policy and the relationships among personnel. Concerns over such matters are not resolved once and for all in a contract. Instead, they require sustained consideration through debate and discussion in an agreed-on forum.

A trust agreement, as part of a teacher union contract, constitutes the definition of the arena for continuing discussion and a focal point for an envisioned outcome. Such issues are not settled by a contract. The trust agreement allows negotiation over policy considerations to continue. Both sides of the negotiation—administration and teachers— continue discussion with the aim of resolving differences over policy matters.

The subject of such ongoing discussions emanating from a trust agreement can be the very structured requisites we have earlier pointed out as needed for restructuring for shared governance: time to meet and discuss, agreements about class size, empowerment of teachers, and school autonomy. Involving a professional union of teachers in a discussion of such managerial issues can provide at least two possible activities central to a learning school: (a) reflective dialogue by participants, thereby stimulating interaction among teacher colleagues, and (b) collaboration among professionals to develop shared values directed at a concerted focus on student learning.

Such trust agreements are no magic formula for successful schools. But in a day of increased collective bargaining between school boards and school administrators, on the one hand, and teachers, on the other hand, trust agreements can facilitate and focus ongoing negotiations for the benefit of increased learning. They have the virtue of keeping alive the important educational policy issues that can easily be lost in the tension and controversy over wages and hours.

Summary

To develop a professional community that focuses on authentic learning, we contend that shared governance is a necessary prerequisite. Instead of a traditional hierarchical model of management, a learning school is characterized by sharing among major stakeholders. At its best, such a professional community has five features: reflective dialogue among participants, deprivatization or interaction among teacher colleagues, a collective focus on student learning, collaboration among education professionals (e.g., administrators and teachers), and shared values and norms.

The research of Louis and Kruse (1995) showed that development of a professional community is a complex process and is not realized overnight. Indeed, it reveals degree differences among professional communities typified as mature, developing, fragmented, and static. The mature community embodies the five features of a professional community on a consistent basis. The developing community shares such features but with less consistency. Although not a totally professional community, it is in the process of becoming one. In contrast, the fragmented community has only partial unity among professionals. Whereas some were apparently intent on reforming the community, others were not. Whether such a situation could move to a developing community is an open question. The static community is one where no one seems able or willing to take the first steps toward a professional community. We would not characterize such a situation as a learning school.

Overall, shared governance is seen not as an end in itself but as a means for moving toward a professional community and a learning school. There are several ingredients that are instrumental for such development. Of prime importance is setting aside time for teachers to meet and discuss common concerns. In turn, structures must be established to facilitate communication among teachers and between teachers and administrators. A consequence of such communication is the deprivatization of teaching. Instead of teaching being a private activity, in a learning school it is a joint activity engaged in by colleagues who provide feedback and formative evaluation to each other.

Leadership in such a context is, to use the phrase of Louis and Kruse (1995), from the center. That is, leadership best comes neither from up high nor from random criticism below. The center is where all participants meet. Leadership is shared. It can originate with the principal. It can emerge from the ongoing discussion among teachers. It can come from the insight of other stakeholders, such as parents, or others from the larger geographic community.

Finally, because in today's school climate teacher unions are playing an important role, we reviewed the research of Kerchner and Koppich (1993) on the educational trust agreement. A trust agreement, growing out of normal collective bargaining, is a mechanism for continuing discussion of vital policy issues. Because it keeps alive important educational questions and can provide a means for their resolution, the trust agreement can be viewed as an extension of shared governance.

Earlier, we highlighted the central importance of the role of vision in educational leadership. In this chapter, we detailed practical steps or ingredients for shared governance. In our view, such shared governance is essential to the vision of a learning school.

7

When Vision Leads
Real-Life Examples

In previous chapters, we have talked about vision from both an individual and a group perspective. A vision, whether individual or shared, is based on a set of values and beliefs. We assert that leaders must possess their own well-articulated personal vision of a school or a school district's future. We believe that this personal vision is important because it serves as the foundation for the development of a shared vision. The role of leaders is to guide other stakeholders to reach consensus and shape their values and beliefs into a covenant of shared values. To guide others, leaders need to have a clear understanding of their own value system. As stated in earlier chapters, leaders do not impose their vision on others. Rather, they create an environment of sustained dialogue where stakeholders share their values and beliefs and ultimately find common ground on which they can build a covenant.

In this chapter, we provide four examples of how leaders engaged others to develop a set of shared values that first became the vision for a school or a district and then became operational in them. We trace the origins of their respective odysseys and, in Chapter 8, glean from their experience some lessons that might be helpful to those about to start on the journey toward developing a new view of what education can be for their schools and their school districts. We begin with examples of three schools that have been in operation for three to four years. We then trace the experience of a school district through the process of developing a shared vision and implementing it.

McCleary School in
Pittsburgh, Pennsylvania

In 1991, the Pittsburgh Public School District needed to reopen two elementary schools that had been closed in the early 1980s. The closed schools were needed to accommodate an increasing elementary school enrollment. At that time, the district was in the process of developing a long-range plan for a school restructuring agenda. A strategy was developed to open these schools as "restructuring schools" to provide the district with firsthand experience related to the restructuring agenda it was developing.

The district developed a request for proposals that encouraged teachers, administrators, parents, and the broader community to prepare and submit proposals to operate these two schools beginning in September 1992. In fall 1991, the district developed guidelines for the proposals and provided orientation sessions and technical assistance to help interested groups formulate proposals. Six teams submitted proposals to operate the two schools. Each of the two chosen teams was funded with monies secured from local foundations and provided by the school district to release a planning team of up to five teachers for the second semester of the 1991-1992 school year. The planning teams had from February 1 to August 31 to prepare for the opening of their schools. Each team had funds to hire consultants and visit other schools or districts to help it execute its vision.

McCleary School, located in the Lawrenceville section of Pittsburgh, was one of the two schools to be reopened. Most of the children who attend the school come from lower socioeconomic backgrounds. The school serves a racially mixed population of approximately 30% African American students and 70 % White or other. The winning concept paper for McCleary School proposed the following as a statement of purpose:

> Our purpose is to envision a school suited to a community of learners. Historically, the idea of community (*communis,* "common") has meant an attempt to find commonality in the diverse situations and backgrounds of individuals. The lives of people of various occupations and stations are woven together in a shared purpose. We envision a school in which children, teachers, parents, and community members all learn matters vital to

their own lives, and where all participants pursue common goals. We envision a school rich in opportunities for discovery learning and community empowerment.

We propose to restructure the McCleary School for grades preschool to five, with an emphasis on technology, cross-age grouping, cooperative learning, and individualization. Literature-based thematic units will involve multiple intelligences and higher-order thinking skills. Our school will embrace a multicultural perspective. The arts will be integrated throughout the curriculum. We will create experiences that engage the total child in "flow" experiences. (McBride, 1991, p. 1)

The concept of *flow experiences,* as described by the winning McCleary proposal team, comes from the writings of Mihaly Csikszentmihalyi (1990). The concept of flow experiences deals, in large measure, with motivation for learning. Flow experiences engage learners in intrinsically rewarding experiences and challenge them to use their knowledge and skills to the limit. The proposal team believed that they could engage students, teachers, parents, and community leaders in creating a learning community that would benefit the entire stakeholder group.

The proposal described the problems with current school structures in relation to the changing conditions in the world and listed assumptions such as the following: "Every child can learn, has a drive to learn, and has a right to learn and to develop all of his or her intelligences. The end of learning is to achieve a happier and more secure life" (McBride, 1991, p. 4).

The proposal stressed the concept of multiple intelligences from the work of Howard Gardner (1988) and placed great focus on the development of analytic thinking and problem-solving skills in students. It also described how the team envisioned the daily lives of children, the involvement of the community, and the professional development of teachers.

Mary Ellen McBride, the concept team coordinator, ultimately became principal of McCleary School. On the basis of her years of experience as a school librarian she had developed a vision of what good education ought to be. In her earlier experience, McBride was the librarian in an all-African American school in Pittsburgh, where she encountered students who were unmotivated and unruly. To remedy the situation she began to build a curriculum based on the children's interests and their motivation to learn. She was highly successful in engaging the students in active learning based on their interests. Later, McBride became the librarian at Brookline Elementary Teacher Center, a professional development school in Pittsburgh, where she was heavily engaged in her own professional development. McBride also became intensively involved in discussion groups with other professionals about school restructuring. Among the many authors she read and discussed with others, at this time, were Howard Gardner (1988), James Comer (1980), and Elliot Eisner (1991). When the request for proposals was issued for McCleary School, she and her colleagues were ready.

The McCleary concept team, led by McBride, was made up of seven teachers, three administrators, a university computer specialist, and a former museum director. The concept team talked with over a dozen community organizations to enlist their support for the development of a school program that would involve the community in significant ways. McBride took on the responsibility of drafting the original proposal for her planning team. The team responded to the draft, and McBride prepared the proposal for submission.

Following notice of the award, McBride and four other teachers, who were members of the proposal writing team, were released from their teaching duties to translate their concept paper (vision) into an operating elementary school. The school opened in September 1992.

As the planning team prepared for the opening, McBride and her planning colleagues were concerned about the need for professional development of teachers who would staff the school. They had the freedom to recruit and select teachers from within the Pittsburgh Public School District but not from outside because of the district's personnel policies, a state-mandated eligibility system for teacher appointments, and the collective bargaining agreement with the Pittsburgh Federation of Teachers.

The major professional development problem, from McBride's perspective, was teachers' inability to combine theory and practice. She found that teachers often do not understand the theory behind the practices they use. McBride believed that, for the school to be successful and for the vision to be implemented with fidelity, teachers would need to have the opportunities to reflect on their practice and to become familiar with the theories that supported the vision the school embraced.

Like most new undertakings, McCleary School struggled during the first year of implementation. Some of the teachers were fearful of departing from traditional instructional practices. They knew what the goals of the school were but were not secure enough to attempt full implementation of the instructional practices envisioned for the school. McBride did a lot of demonstration teaching during the first year; she modeled for teachers the type of teaching practices and student learning experiences that were consistent with the vision for the school.

During the second year, the district received additional funding from local foundations on a proposal jointly prepared with Bank Street College in New York City to conduct ongoing professional development training for teachers at McCleary. The training and consultation offered was highly consistent with the vision for the school as drafted by the proposal team. Much of the training focused on authentic teaching and assessment techniques. By the end of the second year, teachers were much more comfortable using practices consistent with the vision and were engaged in frequent conversations about learning and teaching techniques. The McCleary teachers gained knowledge and confidence in how to engage students successfully in active learning. The training and consultation from Banks Street College continues to this date.

Professional development was focused on enabling teachers to rethink teaching and learning. Teachers worked to develop and implement an integrated social studies curriculum. A major emphasis of the work was to plan the learning experiences that reflected the concept paper's commitment to the idea of multiple intelligences. McBride also placed major emphasis on getting teachers out into the community to use it as a learning resource. One of the goals for students was to allow them to experience the community as a learning tool. During the first year, for example, the students were involved in designing and operating an Italian restaurant in the school. The students engaged in an extensive project to learn about the restaurant business. They visited restaurants, restaurant suppliers, and grocery and department stores. When the students had completed their planning, they purchased all the materials, equipment, and food needed to operate the restaurant, organized a student restaurant staff, and prepared and served meals to their fellow students, parents, and community representatives. This experience exemplifies the project learning experiences provided to pupils at McCleary.

Collaborative management of McCleary is an important vehicle for vision implementation. During the first two years, the union committee in the school was active; however, by the third year the faculty was so involved in shared decision making that union meetings in the school became irrelevant.

As McBride reflects on the influences that shaped the vision and its implementation, she identifies Howard Gardner's (1988) writings as the most influential in the design and implementation of the school. The faculty was also highly influenced by the work of James Comer (1980), particularly as it related to establishing good mental health among the children and their families. Most recently, the faculty has been discussing the work of Elliot Eisner (1991) on qualitative assessment. McCleary has been involved in the development of a set of multiple indicators to demonstrate the impact of the school's program on the student body.

In retrospect, McBride believes that she needed more help with public relations when the school began to operate—and needs it even more today. Many of the messages being sent out early in the school's experience were misinterpreted by parents and the community. For example, rather than talking about themes as the organizing principles for student work, they now use the term *studies*. The concept of themes was misunderstood by parents, somehow carrying with it a connotation of wasting children's time. Now the studies last a full term as opposed to the original themes that lasted two to three months, and the parents accept the studies more readily. Also, compared to the first year, teachers are now better able to effectively articulate to parents the reasons why they are providing certain types of learning experiences for students. However, there is still a great need to engage parents and the public more fully and provide them with a deeper understanding of the school and its vision for their children.

Alice Carlson Elementary and the
Applied Learning Academy in Fort Worth, Texas

Alice Carlson Elementary and the Applied Learning Academy (middle school) in Fort Worth, Texas, represent an interesting story of the creation of schools. These schools were established in response to the community's concern about students' employability upon graduation from high school. Fort Worth is a school district of about 72,000 students, with a student population of approximately 40% Hispanic, 30% African American, and 30% White. In 1991, Don Roberts, then superintendent of the Fort Worth School District, brought together 300 local business leaders to identify the kinds of skills that students needed to be employable upon high school graduation. The business leaders invited to participate ranged from corporate leaders in such organizations as American Airlines to the typical neighborhood grocery store owner. The district used a list of employment skills culled from the literature and developed an inter-view protocol to survey each of the business leaders. Following the administration of the survey and analysis of the data, the business leaders worked with Superintendent Roberts to finalize the skills needed by high school graduates for successful employment in the local economy.

The product that emerged from engaging the business commu-nity was a highly detailed list of "employability skills" that served as the basis for the district's planning for school improvement. Using the data gathered from the survey and the work with the business community, the school district developed an initiative called C^3 (C to the third power) to implement the employment-oriented curriculum. C^3 is an acronym for Corporations, Classrooms, and Community.

Sally Hampton, Coordinator of Writing and Reasoning Skills for the district, assumed the lead role in the planning and implementa-tion of C^3 for writing across the grades and across the curriculum. As Hampton explored the relationship between the kinds of skills that the business leaders identified and the school district's curriculum, she found the district was not preparing students for the real-world job skills identified by the business community. The district had an academic-oriented curriculum that was designed to prepare stu-dents for postsecondary education; the curriculum bore little rela-tionship to the real-world-oriented skills identified by business lead-ers. Hampton discovered that the skills the business community identified were at least as, if not more, demanding of the kinds of thinking skills expected of students preparing for higher education. She discovered that the business community expected students to be comfortable with working with others to solve ill-defined problems. These types of behavior are not characteristic of the academic-oriented learning found in Fort Worth's school curriculum.

Hampton's responsibility in the district, prior to C[3], was to coordinate the development of writing and reasoning skills for students in the district. She worked with teachers and a corps of six writing specialists to train teachers to engage students in effective writing skills. Hampton and her colleagues found that the structure in the district seemed to work against developing meaningful writing skills in students. Hampton began to work with the specialists to explore the literature on apprenticeship and problem-based learning including the Foxfire materials[1] and Sylvia Farnham-Diggory's (1990) book *Schooling*. As Farnham-Diggory states,

> The expertise exists: we know how to design learning environments that nurture mental development and that ultimately produce good thinkers who can reason productively about the cultural, scientific, and technological forces that converge on the lives of citizens of the world and their families. (pp. 196-197)

As they reflected on the district's emphasis on writing and thinking skills for which they were responsible, they found that writing skills sought by the business leaders provided the authentic purpose and the audiences for student writing and thinking. In the real world, students are expected to write brochures, reports, memos, proposals, and the like. The schools must find ways to engage students in writing tasks that they will encounter in the work world.

In general, Hampton and her staff found that the schools needed to involve students in projects for which there were real purposes beyond the school (at least beyond the classroom) and real audiences for their work. From her readings, Hampton began to involve the district's staff in conceptualizing a notion of applied learning.

As the thinking of Hampton and her staff evolved, they came to the realization that, to achieve the goals for applied learning, the district had to create projects for students. These projects would present ill-defined problems for the students to solve, and the projects would culminate in some kind of product. The results of problem solving must have implications beyond the classroom. Hampton and her colleagues decided that learning projects could range from a few days to a year long project.

About the time that Hampton and her colleagues were developing their notions about applied learning, the central administration reorganized and moved from its location in Alice Carlson Elementary to a new building. Hampton asked the superintendent if she could have the empty school for use as a laboratory to create an applied learning school that would test the notions she had been developing as part of the C^3 project. The superintendent agreed to let her have the building if she could convince enough parents to send their children and if she could recruit enough teachers from the district who were willing to try the applied learning approach.

Three town hall meetings were held throughout the community to try to interest parents in sending their children to the school. Although it was not intended to be a magnet school, the applied learning school was designed to draw children from throughout the city. It was agreed that a proportion of the children attending the school would come from the neighborhood in which the school was located. By the time the community meetings were completed, Alice Carlson Elementary not only had a full complement of students but a waiting list trying to enroll. Four years later, the waiting list is huge. Alice Carlson is a K-5 elementary school; a 6-8 middle school—the Applied Learning Academy—was opened to extend the program for the students. And in the fall of 1996, the Applied Learning Academy at Trimble Tech High School opened for ninth graders and will be expanded one grade each year.

Although the staff selected for the school reflected those who were interested in developing the applied learning concept, an extensive professional development program was established for the staff. The professional development program has three stages, and completion of the program is mandatory. The first stage is for entry-level teachers and involves a two-week summer training program. At this level, teachers learn how to set course goals and how to find compelling ideas in the curriculum that can serve as problem-centered, project-learning activities. Teachers are forced to make choices in themes or topics because they will not get the same amount of curriculum coverage as they would in a conventional classroom. Teachers are taught how to design projects and build them around course goals. In the project design phase, care is taken to make sure that real learning occurs for students. Teachers leave the summer session with at least one project ready for implementation during the first year.

Teachers at this initial stage of development are so engaged in learning how to set up projects that it is difficult to focus their attention on the management problems they are likely to encounter during the school year. Hampton and a staff of two people, who now support the schools, meet with teachers on four Saturdays during the school year. During these Saturday sessions, they assist teachers in addressing problems that arise when implementing applied learning. Teachers are required to file an annual report in which they detail what happened during one of the projects implemented that school year.

The second stage of professional development occurs during a two-week session in the second summer. The focus of this session is on problems that arise from a project-driven curriculum and the problems of evaluating student learning. Teachers who do not participate in the training during their first two years of employment in an applied learning school are asked to leave.

Two major problems arise that require attention from professional development. The first relates to the development of projects and evaluation of student learning. The second problem relates to the fact that both teachers and students have higher expectations for learning. As a result, students are learning more than they previously did in the traditional school. A third grade teacher, for example, found that she had to alter her instructional program because students were coming in with advanced skills compared to conventional third graders. Teachers could no longer predict what knowledge and skills students would bring with them from grade to grade. As a result, teachers needed more planning time during the school year than Hampton had initially believed they would need.

Alice Carlson Elementary is addressing the problem of providing more time for teacher planning through a reorganization of the school's administration. Initially, the school had two teacher-directors rather than a principal. When one of the directors retired recently, the remaining director requested that the position not be filled but, instead, be replaced with a floating teacher position. This teacher would work in different classrooms, thus allowing other teachers time to plan curriculum or to observe their coworkers. At this writing, the teacher-director is awaiting approval of the floating teacher.

In recent years, Hampton has spent considerable time working on the New Standards Project to assist the district in developing new assessments of student learning consistent with the vision of the school. Alice Carlson Elementary used a draft version of the standards for the past two years to set course goals and to evaluate student portfolios. However, starting with the 1995-1996 school year, the official version of the standards has been provided by the New Standards Project.

Parent conferences are centered around the standards for student learning. During parent conferences, teachers inform parents of the standards and provide a narrative report of the student's progress toward attaining the standards. Since Alice Carlson Elementary's opening five years ago, the standards have given the school the national reference point that has helped convince parents that the students are learning.

According to Hampton, the parents of Alice Carlson Elementary students expect their children to read and know their multiplication tables. They are pleased that their children are learning and that there are fewer discipline problems. By the time the students are in middle school, however, parents become more concerned about content. The New Standards Reference Exam and the portfolio system contribute to parents' satisfaction that their children are actually learning. Students at both Alice Carlson Elementary and the Applied Learning Academy do better than the district average on state competency tests. This is a significant achievement in view of the fact that the schools have a high percentage of children who experience learning difficulties.

Alice Carlson Elementary and the Applied Learning Academy are governed by councils that involve the teacher-director, parents, teachers, and some students. The schools also have different management teams for different purposes; however, the teachers and the director will turn down any recommendations that distort the school's vision. The only problem that the schools have experienced with parents as council members is their pressure to add a potpourri of programs they have read about. Faculty are concerned that if they respond to parents' desires they would end up with a "Christmas Tree School" filled with a lot of ornaments that don't fit the vision of the school.

The school leaders need to continually remind parents that the focus of the school is on applied learning and that programs cannot be added unless they contribute to the school's goals. It is difficult for some parents to accept this notion. There are even some parents who want Alice Carlson Elementary to identify gifted children and have special classes for them, which the faculty refuses to do. The faculty position is that the curriculum serves all students, including the gifted. It has taken time for the parents to understand fully that teachers and the director will turn down anything that is not consistent with maintaining a cohesive vision for the school.

When asked to describe implementation issues encountered at Alice Carlson Elementary during its early years, Hampton identified several. Teachers initially wanted to stay with students for up to three years beginning in kindergarten. However, primary grade teachers found that not all the teachers had kindergarten certification. A second issue related to the incredible number of people, including parents, who wanted to visit the school. Arranging for visitors and escorting them around the building became an overwhelming problem, solved by each classroom teacher training student docents to escort visitors around the room and explain to them what students are doing and how the curriculum is organized. This solution has given the students an opportunity to build poise and self-confidence.

Hampton now finds herself engaged extensively in public relations work. She spends much time speaking at public meetings and conferences to build support for the applied learning program. Informing other teachers and administrators in the district and helping teachers throughout the district to adopt applied learning strategies also keeps Hampton busy. Approximately 450 teachers in the district have been trained to implement applied learning in their classrooms.

One of the early problems that Hampton had to deal with was convincing parents that children will learn the basic skills in reading, mathematics, and writing. Parents see their children actively engaged in problem solving but are concerned that the children are not "getting all the facts" they need to know. Parents also become concerned with content knowledge and curriculum coverage. Teachers have to assure them that students are learning important facts even though students' use of textbooks is limited. Students use trade books and information from other sources related to the problem they are studying. For example, some Alice Carlson Elementary students were researching information relative to a site being prepared for children's recreation. The students used reading material received from the Army Corps of Engineers about site selection and preparation.

Perhaps one of the most important outcomes of the applied learning schools is that students are happy about coming to school and are highly engaged in learning. Students are very aware of what is expected of them and how their work is graded. Each project has specific rubrics for evaluation. Hampton recalls asking a child what kind of a grade he received on a specific project. The student responded by pulling out the rubric and saying "on a four-point scale, this is a three" (S. Hampton, personal communication, March 15, 1996).

The superintendent has allocated $10,000 to support projects for classroom teachers in the applied learning schools. However, to receive the funds, students must write a proposal that states the goals for the project and includes a budget. Hampton usually visits the class to talk with the students about the goals for their project. One kindergarten class wanted to buy a snake and a hamster for their empty animal cages so that they could observe their behavior. One kindergartner offered to name the animals after Hampton if she would give them the grant. When she revisited the class, the students gave Hampton a complete accounting of their observations of the animals.

In summing up her experience, Hampton speaks of the great pride she has in students:

> I don't know of a group of more self-possessed, articulate young people. They are incredibly capable and resourceful. I am amazed at how much we tend to undermine children's ability to assume responsibility and make decisions. These children are questioning, active, and responsible—and they are having a good time. When you are with them, they are open to sharing their learning with you. Perhaps this type of education is not for every learner or teacher, but it is working at Alice Carlson. (S. Hampton, personal communication, March 15, 1996)

Souhegan High School in Amherst, New Hampshire

The new Souhegan High School in Amherst, New Hampshire opened in 1992 under the leadership of Superintendent Richard Lalley. The school provides a good example of how a committee of stakeholders played an important role in the creation of a vision for a high school. Prior to 1992, Amherst, along with the neighboring community of Mt. Vernon, paid tuition for its secondary students to attend Milford N. H. High School. Amherst had only advisory input regarding the school's operation, and over a period of time, district officials believed that their input was not being taken seriously. Lalley indicated that when issues developed around curriculum, the quality of instruction, or the quality of building maintenance, Amherst's requests to deal with these issues fell on deaf ears.

"Tuition without representation" became a rallying cry for Amherst's collaboration with Mt. Vernon to create a new regional high school with Milford that would share governance among the three towns. A new district was created and a school board elected. The new district tried to pass a bond issue for the construction of the new three-town high school; the permanent status of the regional school union was conditional upon passage of a bond issue. When this bond issue failed to receive the necessary two-thirds majority vote of all three communities, the proposed regional school district was dissolved. Amherst then joined only with Mt. Vernon to form a cooperative high school district, elect a school board, and try to pass a bond issue for construction of the school. This time, with Lalley's leadership, the two communities were successful in obtaining passage of the bond issue, and planning began to construct and open the new high school in 1992.

The school board established study committees of citizen volunteers to help think through the design of the new high school. About 125 volunteers worked on the following committees: curriculum, sports and extracurricular activities, technology, bonding and financing, building, and publicity. The curriculum committee provided the impetus to propose that the school be modeled after the principles proposed by the Coalition of Essential Schools at Brown University.[2] The curriculum committee recommended that the district hire a high school principal who had experience leading a coalition school.

The Curriculum Committee members read *Horace's Compromise* (Sizer, 1984) and *The Shopping Mall High School* (Powell, Farrar, & Cohen, 1985), the latter of which began to open people's eyes to tracking systems in high school that precluded many students from engaging in serious learning opportunities. The committee members did a lot of reading and discussing and decided that the principles espoused by the Coalition of Essential Schools at Brown University most closely mirrored what they thought the community would most value in its public high school.

In addition to the work of the Curriculum Committee, Lalley engaged the school board in a brainstorming session related to these questions: If we had an ideally effective high school, how would we know it? What would be happening? What would be taking place? If we were to visit this new high school five years into its development, what would it look like? What would kids, teachers, and administrators be doing?

What ensued was one of the most fascinating meetings that Lalley ever had with the school board; board members had the same perception. Lalley used a computer that projected what he was keyboarding on a screen; he then keyed in the board members' suggestions so that they could see their responses to the indicators of the high school they wished to see. After the brainstorming exercise, Lalley organized the indicators proposed by the board into the following categories: curriculum, student personnel, finance, management, school and community relations, and so on. Lalley presented this information to the school board members and, following discussion, they agreed that this was the kind of high school they would like to organize.

The results of the school board's brainstorming became input to the Curriculum Committee of the citizens group. The net effect of these experiences was that the community came to agreement that they wanted a reform-oriented high school. As a result, members of the Curriculum Committee studied various reform movements across the country to find what best fit with the desires of the community. The work of the Coalition of Essential Schools was very influential in guiding the work of the committee.

Designing and opening a new high school that would conceptually reflect the values of the community was a significant piece of work. Lalley led the citizen group and the school board to examine how the building would be designed to accomplish the purposes that had been articulated. Rather than take the easy way out by designing the school to reflect traditional high school buildings and then make changes, the citizens decided to rethink every aspect of the school as part of the design process. The goal was to open the new high school with as many reformulated ideas as possible.

One of the important values that permeated the planning of the high school related to student-teacher relations. All participants who were engaged in the planning process believed that current high schools are highly impersonal places for students. Participants believed that large teacher loads prevent teachers from getting to know students well and therefore prevent the crafting of instruction based on a full knowledge of each student's strengths, weaknesses, aspirations, and aptitudes. The entire community became concerned that in a typical high school the students run through a seven- or eight-period day without much person-to-person contact. Amherst and Mt. Vernon residents did not want students to sit through classes day after day, going through a highly impersonal routine schedule. Therefore, the planners decided that teachers in the school should have no more than 80 to 90 students for whom they would be responsible (because of increased enrollment, teachers now have from 85 to 95 students). The plan was to have a core academic team of teachers in English, social studies, mathematics, and science plan for the instruction for a set group of students.

As the school is now operating, the core academic team of teachers has control over how time is to be used for 4½ hours per day; the school controls the remainder of the day. The teams have the freedom to change the schedule on a daily basis to reflect the topic being studied and the interest of students. Time taken away from one subject (e.g., mathematics) is added back in on another day.

Teacher professionalism is the second most important value of the school's program. Teachers are expected to work together closely in their academic teams to design and implement the instructional program for students. Each academic team is provided office space where members can meet to plan, reflect, and analyze their instruction on a daily basis. The school has pledged to treat teachers as professionals and give them the developmental support they need to become critical and supportive friends of one another as they work to provide a quality educational program for students.

The third major value incorporated into the school culture is to have handicapped students previously placed in private residential and day placement centers included, as much as possible, in the life of the high school. It was believed that the newly structured high school could provide a nurturing environment for all students. The school community wanted to instill a shared value that all students have the same heart and mind with similar aspirations for the future. The stakeholders clearly wanted to include, not exclude, handicapped students. The district has received considerable financial support from the New Hampshire Institute on Disabilities to help teachers work with students who have a wide range of impairment and academic ability. Teacher training was provided because the district is committed to the elimination of academic tracking and teachers need to work with mixed-ability groups.

The goal to eliminate tracking in the high school also represents an important value of the Souhegan High School community. Lalley indicates that the district wants to give every student the opportunity to take any course as long as the student meets the prerequisites, if any, and is willing to put forth the effort. Thus, to take an Advanced Placement course, a student must demonstrate the motivation to enroll in the class.

The high school also offers the Honors Challenge, which provides a student with the opportunity to contract with the teacher to perform extra work and earn Honors Distinction. This distinction reflects recognition for academic work that is both quantitatively and qualitatively greater than normal course expectations. The school allows honors work to be documented in any course that a student takes. The requirement is that the teacher and the student enter into a contract to achieve certain goals.

Another guiding principle at Souhegan High School is the Coalition of Essential Schools principle that *less is more*; this value position assumes that studying a topic in depth and thoroughly has more educational value for students than a broad but cursory coverage of topics. Lalley takes the position that the district did not want the community to think that quality education is represented by the number of courses offered in the high school. Rather, the district wanted to eliminate the typical lower-track courses found in most high schools. The goal is to require that all students, not just the best ones, participate in a more rigorous curriculum. In the high school that students attended before the opening of Souhegan, for example, 17 courses were offered in mathematics; Souhegan offers only 7, but all are higher-level courses. The district expects all students to finish three years of integrated mathematics, which is the equivalent of algebra 1 and 2 and geometry.

The values of high expectations for students, elimination of tracking, creation of mixed-ability groups, inclusion of handicapped students, and the elimination of typical lower-track courses form the basis of the vision for Souhegan High School. Lalley indicates that the work of the citizens committee was helpful in laying the groundwork for approval of the program for the high school. He believes that the basic principles of the Coalition of Essential Schools, which the committee proposed for use in the school, were acceptable to the community because they were explained so that the average parent could visualize what his or her son or daughter would be doing by engaging in rigorous schoolwork. Parents were also able to embrace the concept of caring teachers and the fact that students of mixed abilities would be working together. Lalley cites the notion of a senior project or thesis as a culminating activity for seniors as an easy sell. Lalley's ability to articulate the principles of the Coalition of Essential Schools with simple, straightforward illustrations of their application helped him win community approval. Another factor promoting the success of the school is the fact that there is a respect for educators in Amherst that may not be found in other communities.

In retrospect, Lalley believes that the involvement of 125 citizens in helping to frame the values to guide the school was critical. Support from the business community developed, in part, when the school implemented many of the principles of Total Quality Management. The fact that the school developed a compensation system that reflects a teacher's development of proficiency, rather than just length of service, convinced many in the business community that the district was serious about educational reform. Lalley's experience clearly demonstrates the value of engaging the community in the development of a vision for its schools.

In March 1993, a group of citizens placed an article on the school district warrant at the town meeting to reinstate ability grouping, honor rolls, and similar things, but the community voted it down. Lalley believes that the community wanted to give the educators the opportunity to make the reforms work. He also believes that the community's vote of confidence reflects the fact that he kept them fully informed and that they understood and valued what was being implemented in the high school. In addition, the formation of a parent-teacher-student association was instrumental in the school's early years. The association, with excellent leadership, has been able to promote the high school and the involvement of parents in very important ways.

Lalley is sensitive to the fact that the school needs to report to parents on the standard indications of the quality of high school education. Scholastic Aptitude Test scores and Advanced Placement scores are important to parents and the community. The high school reports such indicators as the percentage of students taking Advanced Placement courses, the percentage of students taking a rigorous curriculum, and the like. The data indicate that the number of students taking the Scholastic Aptitude Test has increased to over 90%, and the scores have been rising.

Lalley is currently working with the high school faculty and administration to develop a system of *sensors* to gather data that will help the school and the community monitor the progress of students and the program's implementation. These data will be collected and reported to the community on a regular basis. School personnel also survey parents and students regularly to identify what they like and dislike about the school.

Santa Monica-Malibu Unified School District in Santa Monica, California

Neil Schmidt, superintendent of the Santa Monica-Malibu Unified School District, has led the district through a school restructuring process that has reflected both a top-down and bottom-up strategy. Schmidt believes that, although successful school reform may be mandated initially, reform must come from the inside if it is going to have any life of its own.

Restructuring changes in any school's program or governance in the Santa Monica-Malibu School District requires that 80% of the staff vote affirmatively to support that change; teaching practices and structural changes are included in this policy. One of the essential ingredients to bring about change in the district requires that the public also be involved. This practice is particularly important as it relates to the outcomes of schooling—the quality of student work. "We encourage an emphasis on student work," asserts Schmidt, "not on test scores."

Schmidt points out that changes in school culture take years to accomplish. It takes a long time to create new norms that support significant changes in instruction and student achievement. In Santa Monica-Malibu, two schools have made significant changes in the governance structure and how adults go about doing their work. The students in these schools are actively engaged in the learning process. Additionally, over half the schools in the district are now in the process of creating conditions where significant cultural change can take place.

If the staff in a school can come together on a regular basis and be substantially engaged in reflection to inquire about their teaching practices, change can occur according to Schmidt. Currently, about half of the schools in the district are able to come together three to four hours a day every other week to reflect on their practices. This movement has been supported by a grant from the Annenburg Foundation. The schools involved have had the experience of bringing in a critical friend who has acted as a coach for them as they think through the strategy they wish to pursue.

Although a charismatic principal can do a great deal to initiate the process of school reform, in the final analysis any change requires that the staff work together so that teaching and learning go beyond the four walls of the classroom. One of the norms that must be understood, asserts Schmidt, is the belief that all children bring to the school setting powerful, previous learning experiences that exist irrespective of the conditions in which each child has been raised. Unfortunately, according to Schmidt, many educators believe that some children cannot be truly successful in school because of how they have been raised. The challenge for educational leaders is to break through this barrier and demonstrate to teachers that children do bring powerful learning experiences to school and their job is to access those experiences. The issue becomes one of how to create a set of conditions so that professionals embrace such a belief and their practices reflect this view.

Santa Monica-Malibu Unified School District is made up of about 50% low-income minority students who traditionally do not do well in school. The district also has affluent parents who are very much concerned that there be high expectations placed on the students. Affluent parents worry that heterogeneous groupings of students will lessen the quality of academic demand on their children. Thus, the district is seriously engaged in finding ways to involve the parents and community members in looking seriously at student work so that they can affirm that all students are being challenged.

Schmidt cites the example of Santa Monica High School and its female minority principal. Over a period of several years, this principal has restored the confidence of parents in the high school and brought the faculty together to support some detracking of the curriculum. The key to restoring confidence in the school was establishing very high expectations for students with regard to not only academic achievement but also their general behavior. Currently, Schmidt and the high school principal are in the beginning stages of engaging parents and community leaders in examining and judging the quality of student work as a means of gaining and sustaining public confidence in the school.

The Santa Monica community has been very supportive of Schmidt's efforts to improve the schools. Over $2 million of the city's annual budget is given to the school district to support the schools. The Chamber of Commerce led the effort to increase the amount of taxes for the school district. In general, there is broad community support for improving the quality of education for all students. Community support of the schools is important due to the fact that the district has seen a dramatic shift in its demographics; in 1980, Santa Monica High School was 80% White and 20% minority, compared to today's enrollment of 45% White and 55% minority.

One of the challenges facing Santa Monica-Malibu schools is to convince parents that students need to develop a broad understanding of the subject matter they are studying. Many students score very high on the Scholastic Achievement Test but may lack depth of understanding in the subjects taught in the high school.

Schmidt finds his work in Santa Monica-Malibu very challenging and exciting. With assistance from the Annenburg Foundation and the Coalition of Essential Schools he has found that he has become more thoughtful about his work to improve the quality of education in Santa Monica-Malibu schools.

Summary

In this chapter, we presented four case studies of vision in action. Three of them dealt with the development of a vision for an individual school—McCleary School in Pittsburgh, Pennsylvania; Alice Carlson Elementary in Fort Worth, Texas; and Souhegan High School in Amherst, New Hampshire. The fourth related the story of the Santa Monica-Malibu Unified School District.

In the next chapter, we extract lessons learned from these case studies as we detail ways in which one goes about developing a vision statement for a school or district.

Notes

1. For information on the Foxfire materials, contact Foxfire Fund, P.O. Box 541, Mountain City, GA 30562.

2. Information on the Coalition of Essential Schools is available from Coalition of Essential Schools, Box 1969, Brown University, Providence, RI 02912; telephone 401-863-3384.

8

How to Develop a Vision for Your School or District

In Chapter 7, we presented four case studies that described how vision-based educational leaders created a vision for a school or a district. The essential message of that chapter is that a vision provides the driving force to design the organizational structure and implement learning experiences for students. In this chapter, we briefly review the lessons learned from these four vision-based educational leaders. We also review the development and implementation of a vision and strategic plan in the Beaver Area School District in Beaver, Pennsylvania. The Beaver case study is an example of vision development and its implementations that has evolved over a five-year period.

Because the development of a vision for a school or a district is based on shared beliefs, we present a series of questions that school and community personnel should consider as they clarify the values they wish to embody in their vision. We then present an example of a vision statement developed by the Pittsburgh (Pennsylvania) Public Schools and identify how key concepts embedded in the vision statement can provide the basis for the program and curriculum development.

We then offer for the reader's consideration a model of vision development and vision choice adapted from business and industry. The model developed by Burt Nanus (1992), although produced for business, can be adapted for use by school systems. Finally, we present a series of recommendations for school leaders, parents, community leaders, and residents that will guide the process of vision development.

We begin with a review of vision development exhibited by the four educational leaders presented in the previous chapter.

Lessons Learned From Four Educational Leaders

McCleary School in
Pittsburgh, Pennsylvania

Mary Ellen McBride developed her personal vision of good education as a librarian in a school serving a minority population. She found the need to develop lessons for students, based on student interests, that would actively engage students in learning. Later, as a librarian in a professional development school, the Brookline Elementary Teacher Center in Pittsburgh, she engaged other professionals in expanding her personal vision of the concept of good education through readings and discussions on the topic of school restructuring. In 1991, McBride joined with other professionals and community leaders to actualize their vision through the submission of a proposal to plan and open a restructuring school in the Pittsburgh Public School District.

McBride had developed a clear personal vision of education based on the broad concept of active student learning focused on student interests. As she worked with her colleagues to develop a plan for McCleary School, she broadened her personal vision and it became shared vision with her colleagues. McBride and her colleagues were heavily influenced by the writings of Howard Gardner, Elliot Eisner, and Mihalyi Csikszentmihalyi. McBride and her colleagues developed what Sergiovanni (1994) calls a covenant of shared values (i.e., vision) that guided their work in planning for the opening of McCleary School.

Alice Carlson Elementary School
in Fort Worth, Texas

Sally Hampton had a personal vision of education based on her work as Coordinator of Writing and Reasoning Skills in the Fort Worth Public School District. She became involved in a project with the business community to identify the skills that high school graduates needed for successful employment in the Fort Worth economy.

Hampton then took a leadership role in the district's C³ program (Corporations, Classrooms, and Community). This experience led her to see that skills needed in the workforce were very similar to the reasoning and writing skills she was promoting in the school district. The major difference was that the reasoning and writing skills offered by the school district's traditional academic curriculum were not oriented toward the real world.

Hampton and her colleagues began reading the literature on apprenticeship learning, problem-based learning, and the Foxfire materials. These professional readings and dialogue with her colleagues led them to expand their vision to what is now called *applied learning* in the Fort Worth School District. The concept of applied learning embraces project- or problem-based learning as the primary mode of instruction.

Hampton took the bold step of asking the superintendent to give her the abandoned Alice Carlson Elementary School building so that she could try to implement her vision for applied learning. With the superintendent's approval, Hampton recruited students, a faculty, and administration for the school and began to develop a shared vision of applied learning based on problem-centered pedagogical techniques. The vision evolved as the school expanded to a middle school and now to the opening year of a high school.

Souhegan High School in
Amherst, New Hampshire

Dr. Richard Lalley, Superintendent in Amherst, New Hampshire, led his community and school board to reconceptualize the meaning of a high school education for its youth. Lalley used the creation of a new high school for the region to guide the community and the school board to redesign secondary education.

Lalley engaged 125 community volunteers to rethink the purpose of high school education and make recommendations regarding expectations for students and the organization of the school. The volunteers read extensively about current issues in secondary education and were heavily influenced by the writings of Theodore Sizer and his colleagues in the Coalition of Essential Schools. Lalley engaged the Board of Education in a discussion of what they would envision teachers, students, and administrators doing in the school five years after its opening. Also through discussions with the community, Lalley led it to rethink every aspect of a high school education. The community clearly defined what the school must do for students and faculty to realize its vision for the education of its youths.

Santa Monica-Malibu Unified School District in Santa Monica, California

Neil Schmidt, Superintendent of Santa Monica-Malibu Unified School District, led the district through a restructuring process that reflected a top-down and bottom-up strategy. The bottom-up strategy is important because to implement changes in a school's programs or organization, an affirmative vote of 80% of the school's faculty is required. The top-down strategy is necessary, asserts Schmidt, because the creation of new norms to support active learning for students take a long time to achieve.

Because the school district had experienced significant demographic changes, Schmidt led the faculty and administrators to value the previous learning experiences that students bring to the classroom. He led the professional staff to find ways to access previous student experience and build on those experiences to promote active learning. Schmidt engaged parents and the community in a discussion of student work as a means of affirming that students were being challenged.

The Santa Monica-Malibu Unified School District has been supported in its restructuring effort by a grant from the Annenburg Foundation. The district also embraces many of the principles espoused by the Coalition of Essential Schools.

The Influence of Vision-Based Leadership

In the four cases reviewed above, we see the origin of vision that led the schools or districts evolve from two sources—the individual and the community.

We see, in the cases of both McBride and Hampton, the personal vision of the leader being the driving force for the creation of a new school. Both individuals expanded their personal visions through (a) reading the literature and (b) discussions with their colleagues so that the vision evolved and became shared. The leadership in these two instances, however, emerged from the strong personal vision of each of these educators.

The cases of Lalley, Schmidt, and, to some extent, Hampton portray the involvement of community or staff as the major force to conceptualize or restructure the vision for the district. Lalley used building a new high school to engage the community in a total reconceptualization of secondary education. Hampton used involvement of the business community in defining the skills needed for high school graduates as the foundation for the applied learning program. Schmidt used, among other things, the need to adjust to a new low-income population as one means of engaging faculty, parents, and community in defining expectations for students.

In each of the four cases described in Chapter 7, the power of vision and the effective leadership of administrators in designing and implementing the vision led to successful changes. The vision for the school or the district became shared and valued among the stakeholders. The sharing of the vision in each district became the driving force for its implementation. We now move to an analysis of the vision-building process used by the Beaver Area School District in Beaver, Pennsylvania, to illustrate further the principles of building a vision for a school district.

Beaver Area School District
in Beaver, Pennsylvania

The Beaver Area School District is located in southwestern Pennsylvania, 30 miles from Pittsburgh. The district has a K-12 population of 2,300 students, 50% of whom are classified as rural.

Betty Sue Schaughency was appointed superintendent of the Beaver Area School District in 1991 (she functioned as substitute superintendent in 1990). Schaughency is a career educator in the district having previously served as teacher, guidance counselor, director of guidance, and assistant superintendent. She had the unique opportunity to appoint almost an entirely new central administrative staff in addition to new school principals. Since most of these administrators were new to the district, Schaughency had the task of molding them into a leadership team. She did this by initiating annual summer retreats for the central office and school administrators in 1990. The retreats provided a means of team building and developing consensus on the direction, and the annual plans, for the administration of the district.

Following the first retreat, Schaughency initiated weekly breakfast meetings of the administrative team to build a common knowledge base and develop consensus about their shared values for education and leadership in the district. In the early years, all team members read and discussed, one chapter at a time, the following books: *Control Theory* and *The Quality School* by William Glasser (1984, 1990); *The Seven Habits of Highly Effective People* by Steven Covey (1989); *Quality or Else* by Lloyd Dobyns and Clare Crawford-Mason (1991); and *Leaders: The Strategies for Taking Charge* by Warren Bennis and Burt Nanus (1985). The administrative team also studied the W. Edwards Deming video library (1987) and two of Joel Barker's videos, *The Business of Paradigms* (1989) and *The Power of Vision* (1990). Schaughency's strategy was to engage the administrative team in discussion and reflection on readings and to explore appropriate applications for the school district of what they read and viewed. These breakfast sessions helped bond the administrative team, clarify their vision of education for the common good, and reach a consensus on shared educational and leadership values.

In addition to molding her administrative team, Schaughency held periodic meetings with the school board to build a solid foundation for the future of the school district. Over a period of time, Glasser's (1984) idea of basic psychological needs became the psychological base for the district's mission, and Deming's (1987) 14 Points the theory for its management.

In 1991, she created councils in each school to provide teachers with the opportunity to share leadership-building responsibility with principals. The school councils are an important vehicle to engage the district's faculty in shared decision making. Among other things, the councils react to drafts of the district's annual plans and play a significant role in planning the district's professional development program. In effect, the councils provide a critical mass at the school level to move the district's vision forward.

In fall 1991, teacher members of school councils were trained to lead their colleagues in developing belief statements about education for each school. While schools were each developing their belief statements, Schaughency engaged representative parents and community members in developing their own set of belief statements.

She also engaged members of the Board of Education in the same activity. In spring 1992, representatives of each school staff, the community group, and the Board convened to merge the six sets of belief statements into one set that would serve as a guide for the district. These belief statements would also be used as evaluative criteria to judge the district's implementation of its values. The belief statements are as follows:

We believe . . .

- All people can learn.
- Education involves the development of the whole person.
- Each person has value and deserves to be treated with dignity and respect.
- Individuals reach their fullest potential in a positive learning environment.
- All people are responsible and accountable for their own actions.
- Learning is a lifelong process.
- Education is a team effort involving home, school and community. (Beaver Area School District Strategic Plan, 1993, p. ii)

Schaughency and her administrative team have been significantly influenced by Deming's (1987) theory of management. In fall 1992, the entire professional staff of the district spent a day viewing videotapes of the 14 Points of the Deming Theory of Management and discussing their potential application in the school district (Deming, 1987). Of Deming's 14 Points, the most meaningful to the district are the following: create a constancy of purpose, adopt a new philosophy, institute training on the job, institute leadership, drive out fear, break down barriers between departments, institute a vigorous program of education and self-improvement, and put everyone to work to accomplish the transformation.

Perhaps Deming's most influential idea is his insistence that *profound knowledge* pervades all 14 points. The Beaver Area School District personnel interpret this concept to mean that all people in the system need to have the same, latest information or the same knowledge. Thus, to provide the best knowledge available on relevant topics, experts in their respective fields were brought to Beaver to enhance the learning of the entire staff and community.

Schaughency brought to Beaver futurist David Pearce Snyder, editor of *The Futurist* magazine, and Willard Daggett, Director of the International Center for Leadership in Education, to help inform and validate the strategic planning activities. Snyder and Daggett each spent a day in Beaver talking with district personnel and invited professionals from the region. In the evening, each spoke at an open meeting for corporate sponsors, parents, and community members. These activities, and the discussions that followed, were important in affirming the direction that the district had taken in the planning process.

Snyder focused the attention of the Beaver community on societal and economic trends that would define the world of the 21st century. Daggett challenged the Beaver community to examine the needs of the graduate who will enter the competitive world of work in the 21st century. He stressed the need to have students competent in technical reading and writing, inferential statistics, probability, and problem solving. Above all, Daggett asserted, the competitive worker must know how to apply knowledge. He recommended that the district focus on adult roles for which the graduate must be prepared: citizen, worker, lifelong learner, consumer, family member, and proponent of healthy living. After describing the adult roles, he challenged the district to identify the knowledge and skills that graduates will need to function effectively in those roles.

During fall and winter 1992, the administrative team and school councils engaged all the professionals in the district and about 100 parents and community members in defining the attributes of a graduate of the Beaver Area School District. All participants joined one of seven groups to focus on significant spheres of living as adults. The task given was to identify what an adult needs to know to be able to live a responsible life within each sphere of living. The groups used the following spheres of living to guide their deliberations: personal, relationship, civic, cultural, lifelong learning, and global or environmental. Each group produced a set of responsibilities for each of the spheres (e.g., knows all levels of government and the political process). Then, members of the school councils and the community representatives met to achieve consensus on the definition of the graduate, a significant part of the strategic planning process. The results of the deliberations produced the following definition of the graduate which became the statement of vision for the district and the driving force in strategic planning and its implementation:

> The Beaver Area School District graduate will be well-informed, responsible and prepared for the future:
>> as a CITIZEN whose actions demonstrate high standards;
>> as a COMMUNICATOR who applies the skills of reading, listening, researching and writing, speaking, and presenting;
>> as a WORKER who uses technology, cooperates, and strives for quality;
>> as a THINKER who uses the skills of reasoning, problem-solving, and decision-making;
>> as a LEARNER who is self-directed and creative;
>> as an INDIVIDUAL who strives to maintain good health, to relate well with others, and to enjoy life. (*Beaver Area School District Newsletter*, 1993b, p. 1)

The definition of the graduate is the vision for the Beaver Area School District and the statement of supporting beliefs its philosophical foundation. Armed with these important statements, Schaughency, the administrative team, and the school council members led the district through a comprehensive strategic planning process during spring and summer 1993.

Although each school developed priorities for improvement, the major focus was systemic reform of educational programs and services, kindergarten through Grade 12. The planning design included the following: (a) discern the future, (b) define the graduate, (c) develop standards, benchmarks, and assessments, (d) design learning experiences, and (e) determine instructional strategies.

Nine additional strategic planning committees were established, with the following purposes identified for each:

> 1. *Community Communications:* To improve the process of two-way communication between schools and the community.
> 2. *Community Recreation:* To study possible ways to expand leisure opportunities for the community, particularly youth.
> 3. *Community Wellness:* To engage individuals and groups in activities which promote healthy lifestyles.
> 4. *Facilities and Grounds:* To study long-term needs for facilities and grounds to support the educational programs and activities.

5. *Finance:* To study the financial status of the school district and to make long-term projections.

6. *Institute for Leadership:* To establish a permanent forum to study, to discuss, and to improve leadership.

7. *Policy Review:* To review and to recommend updates in school district policies to the Board of School Directors.

8. *School District Partnerships:* To establish mutually beneficial links between the school district and other organizations.

9. *Technology:* To study ever changing technology and to make recommendations to the buildings and grounds committee about technological updates. (*Beaver Area School District Newsletter,* 1993a, pp. 4-5)

Nearly 200 parents worked with school officials and members of the Board of School Directors to complete development of the strategic plan. The final product, covering the years from 1993 to 1999, was filed with the Pennsylvania Department of Education in September 1993. Then the work of implementation began in earnest.

The completed strategic planning process was committed to the continuous quality improvement of the entire school system. The district's basic premises about the restructuring of schools are expressed in the following assumptions:

- The focus of improvement efforts must be the entire system, not its parts.
- The *system* is the entire school community, i.e. students, staff, parents, school directors, taxpayers, organizations, businesses and other community members.
- The foundation is our *belief statements,* enabling us to gauge our behavior for congruence.
- The internal *customer* (client) is the student; external customer: parents, taxpayers, employers, higher education and society.
- The product is *education.* We set the conditions for success in the educational programs and services we provide.
- The vision is the *graduate,* who is successfully prepared for the future.
- The system cannot be impacted without the involvement of everyone in acquiring knowledge, in decision-making, and in implementation.

- Leaders must understand and demonstrate a more comprehensive form of leadership than has been expected in the past.

- We must acquire the best knowledge available before making decisions. We will explore, select, train and implement.

- We have begun a journey of continuous learning and a commitment to continuous improvement by everyone in the system. (*Beaver Area School District Strategic Plan*, 1993, p. 3)

Work to implement the Beaver Area School District's strategic plan is progressing. The first two stages of the plan to restructure educational programs and services—discerning the future and defining the graduate—were completed early in the process.

Teachers are engaged in systematic professional development training to assist them in achieving the district's vision. During the 1994-1995 academic year, the district focused on an alternative assessment of student learning after the staff realized that they knew very little about the topic. All teachers received a copy of Richard Stiggins's (1994) book *Student-Centered Classroom Assessment* to develop a common frame of reference for student assessment. Teachers participated during the year in 10 days of professional development training planned by a lead group of teachers. Richard Stiggins worked with the entire staff on one of these days. Teachers at all levels of the district now report that they have reconceptualized their idea of student learning and how to assess it. Teachers acknowledge, however, that much remains to be learned.

As a result of their study of various kinds of assessments, the district's professionals decided to develop in 1995-1996 a portfolio system from kindergarten to Grade 12. The portfolio system was designed to make connections from grade level to grade level and across the disciplines, and it encompasses not only students as learners but also professionals as learners. Teacher groups have developed portfolio handbooks for students, faculty, and parents. Currently, work is progressing on developing performance standards for each of the academic disciplines and on developing standards across the disciplines for the graduate proficiencies. Professional development training will continue to assist teachers in generating content and performance standards since the standards and the concomitant assessments heavily influence the final two phases of restructuring—learning experiences or curricula and instructional strategies.

As the district revises its curricula and instructional strategies, it will address such issues as multiple intelligences, learning styles, and flexible scheduling. This phase of development and implementation includes real-life applications of learning and how the learning is assessed.

The Beaver Area School District describes itself as a learning organization reaching into a learning community. The process described above provides a model for bringing a community together to envision the future for its children. It also provides a model for engaging professionals and the community in planning to reach that goal. It is the vision of the graduate that drives all planning, development, and assessment activities. The belief statement acts as a template to keep all parties focused on behaving in a manner consistent with their values. It is the basic assumptions about the restructuring process that communicate a seriousness of purpose. The mission statement for the Beaver Area School District expresses its values well: "Our mission is to create and sustain a school community consistent with our belief statements in which all students will be well-informed, responsible and prepared for the future as: citizens; communicators; workers; thinkers; learners; and individuals" (Beaver Area School District, 1995).

The work proceeds in Beaver to align curricula and instructional strategies with the vision and belief statements and the assessment strategies. As Schaughency continues with the implementation of the strategic plan for the district, she will have brought the vision for the district to its fulfillment in the classrooms and in the community. Though it will take several more years to achieve the full implementation of the district's plan, significant progress has been made to provide a viable model for other districts to adapt.

How to Build a Vision Statement

Identifying Your Values and Beliefs

Central to the building of both a personal vision and a shared vision is the clarification of your core values. What you and your colleagues believe, value, and are willing to act upon forms the basis of your vision. In turn, your vision becomes the driving force to develop a strategic plan for implementation; the vision statement provides the template to ensure that instructional and assessment practices are internally consistent. Additionally, your vision influences how a school should be organized and helps to clarify the policies, practices, and governing structure of the school.

The following questions provide the basis for both reflection and dialogue to achieve the development of both a personal and a collective vision for a school or school district: What is learning? What is teaching? What is knowledge? What is assessment? What is the role of a teacher? What is the role of a student? What is the role of curriculum? What is the role of instructional materials? What is the role of technology? The answers to these questions form the basis for the development of both your personal vision and a shared vision for a school or district.

In all probability, you will need to stimulate your personal reflection and dialogue with your colleagues by engaging in professional readings that will help you clarify and sharpen your values and beliefs. Among other questions that might be helpful in reflection and dialogue are the following:

- What is the importance of skill development, attitudes, and habits in your vision of education?
- What value do you place on developing interpersonal skills, problem-solving or inquiry skills, team learning, and independent study skills?
- What is the role of learning how to learn, developing the habits of lifelong learning, and thinking about how you learn (metacognition)?
- What is your position on active learning, authentic assessment, and portfolio evaluation? What is your position on relating learning to the world outside school?
- What should students know about the structure of academic disciplines?
- Should curriculum be organized for broad coverage, or for in-depth study of a few selected topics? Should the curriculum be organized to reflect interdisciplinary learning? Should the curriculum be organized to reflect racial, ethnic, and gender issues?
- To what extent and how should the learning environment reflect a concern for the self-worth of students?

- To what extent and how can the learning environment promote student gratification in learning?

The Role of Professional Reading

The questions listed above only begin to scratch the surface of the issues, values, and beliefs that you and your colleagues need to discuss as you evolve toward the development of the vision that will guide your leadership. Remember that it is important that the dialogue be an informed one. As you engage in discussion to share your values, it is important to inform the discussion with the latest research, theory, and practice related to the issues you discuss. Having members of a group read and discuss strong professional literature is a good way to stimulate thoughtful dialogue. In the cases previously cited of McBride, Hampton, Lalley, and Schaughency, the participants gained significant insights from readings that helped them come to a consensus on a vision. The development of a vision and its continual refinement based on experience is a long process that requires a significant amount of discussion. The creation of a learning organization requires individuals to be thoughtful about their policies, practices, and beliefs and the impact of them on the organization.

The Nanus Model of Vision Development

Burt Nanus (1992) in his book *Visionary Leadership* states the importance of vision forcefully: "There is no more powerful engine driving an organization toward excellence and long-range success than an attractive, worthwhile, and achievable vision of the future, widely shared" (p. 3).

If a vision is attractive to constituents, they will commit time and energy to achieve it. If it is worthwhile, it will create meaning in the lives of the participants and clarify the purpose and the mission of the organization. If the vision is achievable, it will bridge the past and the future and be realistic. It will be perceived as being a realistic extension of the current state of the organization.

Although the Nanus model for vision development was created for business and industry, it does have relevance for educators. He states that powerful and transforming visions have the following properties:

They are appropriate for the organization and the times;

They set standards of excellence and reflect high ideals;

They clarify purpose and direction;

They inspire enthusiasm and commitment;

They are well articulated and easily understood;

They reflect the uniqueness of the organization;

They are ambitious. (pp. 28-29)

Nanus developed a four-step process for the selection of a vision of an organization that we have adapted for use by a school or a school district. The Nanus model for vision development has four stages: audit, scope, context, and choice. Each is discussed below as it relates to educational organizations.

The purpose of the *vision audit* is to develop a full understanding of the current state of the school or school district. The vision-building process begins with a review of the mission of the school or district. Remember that a vision is a mental image of the future of a school or district. The mission is its purpose, which generally is to prepare students for higher education, a productive work life, and effective citizenry. The vision provides clues as to how the school or district will fulfill its purpose. In conducting the vision audit, it is important to (a) clearly identify the school or district's current operating policies and values and (b) review its current vision, if it has one.

The purpose of the *vision scope* is to identify the school or district's key stakeholders and their needs and to begin to target the vision. The stakeholder analysis causes one to examine the five to six most important constituents of the school or the district such as students, parents, taxpayers, teachers, the business community, and so forth. Having identified these stakeholders, it is important to elicit the major expectations that they have for your school or district. Nanus (1992) suggests that you identify the threats or opportunities that arise from an analysis of stakeholder concerns. For example, if some of the constituents are concerned about school choice, charter schools, or high taxes, these concerns need to be considered as you develop your vision statement.

In targeting your vision, Nanus recommends that you identify any constraints that may influence your vision development process. These might be time, geographical, or social constraints. Another important aspect of targeting the vision is to identify the success criteria that will be used to judge successful vision implementation. In the case of the Beaver Area School District, the development of performance indicators provided the success criteria to judge the attainment of the vision.

The purpose of considering the *vision context* is to help you think about forces operating in your community and to ascertain how these forces might influence the ultimate choice of your vision. Among the forces that you need to consider, according to Nanus, are the following:

- What major changes might be expected in the needs and wants of your constituents?
- Are there likely to be any significant changes in the major stakeholder groups?
- Are there likely to be any significant economic changes in the future (e.g., plant closing)?
- What, if any, changes might occur in the social environment (e.g., higher crime rate)?
- What changes might occur in the political environment (e.g., election of governor hostile to public education)?
- What major changes might there be in technology? (Nanus, 1992, pp. 84-96)

Nanus suggests that you estimate the probability of occurrence of each of the forces that you identify as potentially influencing your vision choice. Appendix A provides an analysis of probability statements developed by a group of students in the Superintendents Academy at the University of Pittsburgh. While enrolled in the Vision-Based Educational Leadership course, these students applied the Nanus model to the selection of a vision choice for the mythical Three Rivers School District. The results of their deliberations are reported in Appendixes A, B, and C.

Another part of the Nanus process of examining the vision context is to write three or four scenarios that describe alternative future visions for your school or school district. Each scenario should represent a theme that reflects a vision choice. The scenario presented in Appendix B reflects one potential vision choice for the mythical Three Rivers School District. Having completed these scenarios, you are in a position to evaluate each scenario in relation to the current strengths and weaknesses of your school or district.

Nanus (1992) describes *vision choice* as a process of putting it all together and deciding on a course of action to pursue. It requires you to synthesize the results of the analyses of the vision audit, scope, and context. He suggests that you take the scenarios developed for the vision context and ask the following questions (p. 121):

- To what extent is the potential vision future oriented?
- To what extent is it *utopian*, or likely to lead to a better future for the school or school district?
- To what extent is it *appropriate*—does it fit with the school or district's history, culture, values?
- Does it set high standards and reflect *high ideals*?
- Does it *clarify purpose* and direction?
- Will it *inspire enthusiasm* and commitment?
- Does it *reflect the uniqueness* of the school or district?
- Is it *ambitious* enough?

Nanus then suggests that each of the alternative visions for the school or district be rated on a scale from 1 to 5 (with 1 the lowest value) for each of the questions listed in the previous paragraph (see Appendix C, Table 1). He then suggests that each of the criterion questions listed in the previous paragraph (e.g., utopian) be given a relative weight on a scale from 1 to 10 (with 10 the highest value). Next, multiply the weight of the criterion by the "goodness" of the scenario (see Appendix B). For example, if the scenario in Appendix B (authenticity) is given a rating of 5 on future orientation and that criterion question is given a relative weight of 10, the score for the scenario on authenticity is 50 (see Appendix C, Table 2). Other scenarios dealing with vision alternatives such as quality community education, ungraded or untracked schools, and charter schools are not included in the appendixes; however, they are identified as vision alternatives 2, 3, and 4, respectively, in Appendix C, Tables 1 through 7.

Nanus (1992) then suggests that measures of success be established for the school or district and that each of the scenarios be rated on the extent to which it might attain the success criterion. Success criteria might include the following: enhanced student achievement, enhanced school completion rate, or enhanced faculty and student morale. Each of the scenarios is rated against the success criteria on a scale from 1 to 5 (see Appendix C, Table 3). Nanus suggests that each success criteria be given a relative weight on a scale from 1 to 10 for each scenario; the score for the success criteria is then multiplied by the relative weight of the criteria. For example, if the scenario on authenticity is given a rating of 5 for the criterion of increased school completion rate and the relative weight of that criterion is 10, the result is a score of 50 for the authenticity scenario. Rating each of the scenarios on measures of success multiplied by the relative weight of each criterion and the products then summed produces a total score for each scenario (see Appendix C, Table 4).

The Nanus model then calls for stakeholders to identify variables that reflect the organization's synergy. The purpose is to rate each of the vision scenarios against a set of criteria that reflects key variables such as the organization's culture and values, strengths, and the needs of the stakeholders (see Appendix C, Table 5). Again, Nanus suggests that each of the criteria for organizational synergy be rated on a scale of 1 to 10 and that the score given to each variable on each vision alternative be multiplied by its relative weight and summed to get a total score for each vision alternative (see Appendix C, Table 6). Finally, he suggests that the totals from Tables 2, 4, and 6 be summed to achieve an overall score for each of the vision alternatives (see Appendix C, Table 7).

The Nanus model may appear to some to be a mechanical or overly analytic process. However, it does make the vision choice process a reasonably objective one and does yield a score for each scenario. It causes the stakeholders to consider contextual and organizational variables that may significantly influence the choice of a vision for a school or district. The results of the analysis can then be used by the educational leader and the stakeholders to make a final choice of a vision to pursue. The Nanus model, adapted for education, is designed to provide a degree of objectivity in the process of selecting a vision for a school or district. The stakeholders of the school or district will take these data into account, in addition to other sources of information, when making the final decision on the vision choice. The results of the analysis should inform the decision-making process but not necessarily control it.

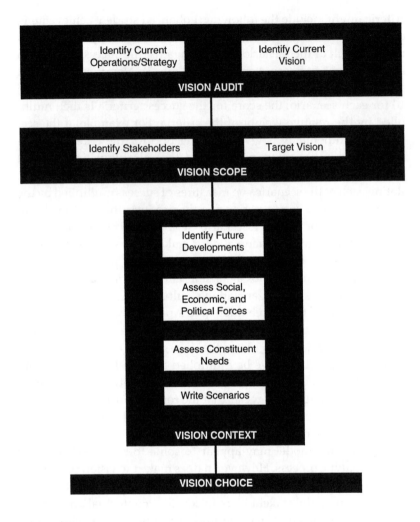

Figure 8.1.

A diagram of the Nanus vision choice process is presented in Figure 8.1. The Nanus vision choice model provides a stakeholder group with a model to develop and select a vision choice and then use that choice to develop the strategic plan to implement the vision. To provide another perspective on vision-based educational leadership, we turn to a vision statement developed by the Pittsburgh Public Schools to guide its strategic implementation plan for school restructuring.

Pittsburgh (Pennsylvania) Public Schools Vision Statement

The Pittsburgh Public Schools submitted its strategic implementation plan to the Pennsylvania Department of Education in January 1995. The plan had evolved over a period of three years as the district engaged more than 500 stakeholders in the process. The Strategic Implementation Plan for Restructuring represents the blueprint for preparing students for the 21st-century workforce. The plan focuses on five structures: high standards for all students, effective schools, dynamic parent or guardian and community partnerships, highly qualified staff and effective volunteer partnerships, and school-based decision making—aligning resources with student needs. The following are its statements of mission and vision:

Mission

The mission of the Pittsburgh Public Schools is to educate every young person to contribute responsibly to our changing society and world.

Vision

Our schools are places where all students learn and thrive in a safe environment where they are respected and valued. Our schools foster a love of learning equipping all students with skills, tools, knowledge and understanding to live, play, and work successfully in the new and different world of the twenty-first century.

Our schools are places of hope for all students, places where cultural diversity and individual differences are appreciated, and where all students achieve their potential.

In our schools, the entire community participates with our students as partners, helping them to become lifelong learners as they grow toward adulthood. Educators, parents or guardians, community organizations, businesses, colleges, and universities all contribute to nurture and develop the talent of our students.

With this support, our students learn to think, solve problems, create, reason, evaluate and make responsible decisions. They are successful in human relationships and contribute to the well-being of our diverse, democratic society. (Pittsburg Public Schools, November 1995)

Readers should remember that a mission statement expresses the purpose of the organization; a vision statement provides a mental image of the future of the school district. The careful selection of words in the Pittsburgh vision statement provides the basis for the development of programs, initiatives, and a strategic plan that will enable the district to move toward the attainment of its vision for students and the community.

The first paragraph of the Pittsburgh statement includes the key words *safe environment, respected,* and *valued.* These words convey the impression that the district will work to provide a safe learning environment within a dynamic urban community. It further states that all students will be respected and valued. The district must translate these values so that the verbal and nonverbal behavior of its teachers, administrators, and staff communicate to students, parents, and others that they are accepted and respected. The key variable of respect for the person, rights, and responsibilities of students and others, when fully implemented in a school or a school system, creates a climate of trust to support student learning.

The words *skills, tools, knowledge,* and *understanding* in the first paragraph communicate the district's commitment to provide students with what they need to *live, play,* and *work* in the world of the 21st century. In achieving these goals, the district intends to develop in students a *love of learning.* The district's strategic plan places emphasis on creating developmentally appropriate instruction for all students with an emphasis on active learning strategies to promote a love of learning.

The second paragraph expresses the values of *hope, cultural diversity,* and *individual differences.* These values communicate the intent of the district to respect and honor the contributions of the different racial and ethnic groups that attend the schools. The statement also endorses respect for individual differences across a range of student abilities from students who may be physically or mentally handicapped to those who are gifted in a variety of ways. The value of hope communicates to children of poverty that working hard to achieve a good education provides them with the hope of a better future.

The third paragraph of the statement envisions the entire community in Pittsburgh working with the schools to achieve the vision for the district. All stakeholders need to work together to provide a high quality of life for the city's residents and the business community as well as a high-quality education for its children and youths. This part of the vision statement is reflected in the strategic plan where all elements of the community find ways of working together to support the education of students to a high level of learning and accomplishment.

The final paragraph expresses the value that students will learn to *think, solve problems, create, reason, evaluate,* and *make responsible decisions.* It also envisions students as being *successful in human relationships.* These values require that the school district provide learning experiences that promote critical thinking and problem solving. It further requires that students be given opportunities to create products that demonstrate the new knowledge they have created for themselves. Finally, the vision statement indicates that the district has a responsibility to provide students with interpersonal skills that enable them to live and work together effectively in the school environment, their community, and the world of work. Among other things, this statement means that the schools have to prepare students to engage in productive problem solving and conflict resolution.

The Pittsburgh Strategic Implementation Plan for Restructuring was formally adopted by the Board of Education, and its implementation began in the 1995-1996 school year. The plan includes appendixes that specify the student learning outcomes to be attained. We now turn to a brief discussion of the need to translate the elements of a vision statement into behaviors in which stakeholders engage when implementing a vision.

Behavioral Correlates
of a Vision Statement

Vision statements such as those from the Beaver Area School District and the Pittsburgh Public Schools require further elaboration and definition to be fully implemented. Vision statements in and of themselves can be viewed as mere platitudes. They take on meaning only when they are carefully analyzed and result in descriptions of what students, teachers, administrators, and others will actually do to achieve the values explicit in the vision. Unless the stakeholders have an operational understanding of the values expressed in the vision statement (in terms of actual behavior) and make a commitment to implement those values, a vision statement is not worth the paper on which it is printed. It is unfortunate that many schools and institutions believe that a vision statement can be created by a few people, committed to writing, and pulled off the shelf when someone asks about its vision. The reality is that a vision statement must become a living document that guides the stakeholders to reflect on their values and evaluate whether or not their behavior is consistent with their espoused vision. A vision statement must also be periodically reviewed and revised based on experience encountered in implementing it. In the Beaver Area School District, for example, the definition of the graduate and the beliefs that support it are prominently displayed in all schools. They are constantly used as criteria to judge whether the actions and achievement of students and stakeholders are consistent with the vision and the beliefs.

One of the most important activities that principals and superintendents can undertake is to examine the policies and procedures of the school or district to make sure they support and are consistent with the vision. The actions and behaviors of stakeholders in the school or district must speak as loudly as the words.

Which Method Should I Follow in Developing a Vision?

It doesn't matter what method or process a leader and stakeholders follow in developing a vision for a school or district. Whether you attempt to quantify the process as Nanus (1992) does or whether you follow a process similar to what Schaughency used does not really matter. What does matter is that the process be one that requires substantial discussion about the questions that are of most concern to the stakeholders. These questions should be similar to those that Nanus raised: Is the proposed vision a good fit with the history of the organization? Is the proposed vision one to which key stakeholders can commit? Will it energize them? Does it set high standards? These and other questions will help the stakeholders reach a reasoned decision about the direction in which the district should move.

We suggest that those engaged in the process of vision building do the following:

1. Develop at least two to three vision alternatives for the school or the district. Developing realistic alternative futures for the

school or the district will sharpen the thinking of the participants and will likely lead to the selection of an alternative that has a good chance of being successful.

2. Clarify the assumptions that underlie your vision or belief statements. What are the assumptions that you are making about learning, teaching, and so forth?

3. Be sure that the elements of your vision statement are internally consistent with one another.

4. Be sure that you have identified and analyzed the current forces operating in your community that may influence the implementation of your vision (e.g., economic, political, or social forces) and estimate the impact they may have on vision implementation.

5. Estimate the extent to which your constituencies for the vision (students, parents, taxpayers, teachers, administrators) will support its implementation.

6. Examine the existing policies, procedures, and practices for their consistency with the vision (e.g., to what extent are the policies, procedures, and practices of the district likely to support a vision of school-based decision making?).

7. Don't rush the process of developing a vision. Take the time to ensure that all stakeholders understand what you are trying to achieve and understand the implications of the vision statement for budget, policy formulation, instructional, and administrative practices.

8. Recognize that it will take a considerable amount of time to reach consensus on a vision statement. Once the vision statement is agreed on, it will take time to develop a strategic plan to implement the vision. And it will take three to five years to fully implement the vision once the plan has been developed.

Summary

This chapter provided the reader with insights about the origin of vision statements. We reviewed how each of the educational leaders described in Chapter 7 went about the process. Both Mary Ellen McBride of McCleary School in Pittsburgh and Sally Hampton of

Alice Carlson Elementary School in Fort Worth used their own personal vision of education and built a shared vision with colleagues. Richard Lalley of Souhegan High School and Neil Schmidt of Santa Monica-Malibu Unified School District used the conditions in the community as the basis for developing a vision for schools.

Betty Sue Schaughency of the Beaver Area School District engaged the community in discerning the future, defining the graduate, and eliciting beliefs. She then led the professional staff to develop the evaluative criteria to judge the fulfillment of the vision. Currently, the Beaver Area staff is busy developing authentic assessments and aligning curricula and instructional strategies with the vision.

We then proposed a series of questions that could be used to begin thinking about the values and beliefs that must support any vision statement. The Nanus model was presented as one vehicle to engage a stakeholder community in a specific process to develop a vision choice. We ended the chapter with a series of recommendations that an individual or a group might use when developing a vision statement for their school or district.

9

From the Learning School to the Learning Community

We have presented the learning school as a place where students engage in active learning that prepares them to become lifelong learners and problem solvers. The type of learning that we espouse in the learning school is called meaning making—the type of learning in which students create new knowledge for themselves. Our perspective on learning reflects a constructivist perspective (see Chapter 3). However, we do not mean that students create knowledge only by themselves. For students to engage in disciplined inquiry (Newmann & Associates, 1996) they must access the bodies of knowledge that form the traditional academic disciplines.

The role of the teacher in the learning school is to strike a balance between dissemination of information and engaging students in actively seeking answers to questions the teacher or student formulates. Obviously, the student must acquire the tool skills of learning—reading, writing, calculating—to engage in active learning experiences. Our vision of students in the learning school is one where they are actively engaged with each other and with teachers in pursuing answers to questions posed for them and by them. We also envision that community resources are used extensively in the learning process as we relate school learning to the real world.

The learning school is also a place where teachers engage in lifelong learning to expand their pedagogical skills, thus enhancing their impact on student learning. Teachers become students in the learning school when they gather data on student performance, visit each other's classrooms, and take collective responsibility for student learning (see Chapter 6). The principal in the learning school takes responsibility for creating and fostering the conditions that promote continuous teacher professional growth. Of course, the principal also assumes the general responsibility of creating the support conditions that enable teachers and students to pursue effective learning.

We also envision that the learning school engages the entire community in the process of providing effective student learning. Parents, community leaders, and senior citizens all work together to support the school and assist students in reaching the goals of becoming lifelong learners and productive citizens.

What we have described above are the elements of a learning community. A learning community, according to Thomas Sergiovanni (1994, p. 164), is one where all stakeholders engage in a quest for shared meaning. In this chapter, we review the concept of a learning organization as described by Peter Senge (1990) in *The Fifth Discipline,* and we also review features of a learning community described by Sergiovanni (1994) in *Building Community in Schools.* We compare the major concepts of Senge and Sergiovanni with Louis and Kruse's notion of the professional community (see Chapter 6) and then cite examples from the case studies in Chapters 7 and 8 where the broader community was engaged. Finally, we provide some guidelines that schools or districts might use to engage the broader community in building and maintaining a learning community.

Senge's Learning Organization

The work of Peter Senge and his associates is well known in the fields of management and education. Senge is the director of the Systems Thinking and Organizational Learning Program at the Sloan School of Management, Massachusetts Institute of Technology. The work of Senge and his colleagues began with attempts to make dysfunctional business organizations more effective. In doing so, Senge studied organizations that have become effective and identified the key variables that are likely to improve an organization's performance. Many educators have found Senge's ideas central to developing more viable working conditions for teachers and school administrators and for improving the quality of education for students.

The basic concept of a learning organization is defined by Senge (1990) as "an organization that is continually expanding its capacity to create its future" (p. 14). Not only does the learning organization engage in adaptive learning as it adjusts to new situations, it engages in generative learning to create new structures and procedures to move the organization to a higher level of performance. We believe these ideas are central to the development of the learning school.

Senge and his colleagues describe the development of a highly creative learning organization as a team of people who work well together and produce a high level of achievement. In the process of developing a great team and moving toward the development and implementation of a shared vision, each team member gains new knowledge and skills that enable them to achieve higher levels of performance. Team members learn from one another as they learn to create new and more effective ways of doing things. Accordingly, Senge describes the effective team in a learning organization:

> Over time, as people start to see and experience the world differently, new beliefs and assumptions begin to form, which enables further development of skills and capabilities. This deep learning cycle constitutes the essence of a learning organization—the development of not just new capacities, but of fundamental shifts of mind, individually and collectively. (Senge et al., 1994, p. 18)

For Senge and his colleagues, the learning organization is one in which the members engage in deep learning that demonstrates effective use of five disciplines: personal mastery, shared vision, mental models, team learning, and systems thinking. We review each of the disciplines and relate them to the creation of the learning school.

Personal mastery means that all people in the school as a learning organization understand that they have a responsibility to contribute to its overall effectiveness. Individuals realize that they must work as members of a team that will bring the school to new levels of achievement for students, adults, and the community. Personal mastery means that all individuals commit themselves to becoming the best possible professionals and team members that they can be; they make a commitment to their colleagues to improve the quality of work life for themselves and the quality of teaching and learning for students.

Shared vision is the essence of this book. Through an emphasis on personal mastery, members of the school community continually seek to clarify and share their individual and collective beliefs and values that form the core of the vision for the school. Shared vision is not a static thing; it is not necessarily a document (we believe that it should be a reasonably short statement) but can be a mental image of the future of the school widely shared by the participants. Vision is dynamic—it is continually being refined as it influences the behavior of all the stakeholders of the organization.

Mental models are the unspoken norms that govern how the school operates. They describe "how things are done around here." Often, these mental models are never brought to the surface and examined for what they do, or do not do, for the learning school. To achieve maximum productivity for all stakeholders, the mental models that influence how things get done in the school need to be examined to ensure that they are consistent with the shared vision for the school and the beliefs that stakeholders espouse. The main question that stakeholders must ask is are the rules, regulations, and procedures for operating our school consistent with our espoused beliefs, practices, and vision?

Team learning refers to the capacity of the stakeholders to reflect on the functioning of the learning school. It is important for teachers and administrators to engage in sustained reflection on the impact of classroom structures, time schedules, pedagogical techniques, assessment, and the like on student learning. It is equally important for team members to critically examine the effects of the above elements' interaction on their own professional performance and growth. Team learning, successfully implemented in the learning school, engages parents and community members in reflecting on the collective impact of all their actions on attaining the shared vision of the school.

Systems thinking, simply stated, means that members of the learning school are able to "see the forest for the trees." That is, members of the learning community are predisposed to see individual actions or activities in relation to the entire operations of the school. Systems thinking means that members of the learning school are predisposed to examine the relationships of the part to the whole; they recognize that modifying one element of the school will affect other elements of its operations. Systems thinking is, in many respects, a mind-set; it is a disposition to constantly look for part-whole relationships.

The five disciplines of the learning organization when applied to education simultaneously influence school organization, interpersonal and group relations, and the capacity of stakeholders to re-invent schools to be more effective. Although each of the disciplines has its own purpose and value, it is the interaction among them that creates the organizational dynamics to improve the effectiveness of the learning school. The learning school must be a reflective community that seeks continual improvement of the organization and its impact on its clients—students, parents, and the broader community. This brief exposition on the learning organization does not do justice to the concept. For an in-depth discussion of the concepts, readers are referred to Senge's (1990) *The Fifth Discipline* and Senge et al.'s (1994) *Fifth Discipline Fieldbook.*

Sergiovanni's Learning Community

For another perspective on the learning organization and the learning school, we turn to Thomas Sergiovanni's (1994) *Building Community in Schools,* where he forcefully asserts that "it is time that the metaphor for the school was changed from formal organization to community" (p. 14).

A community is bound together by shared values, ideas, and commitments, according to Sergiovanni; organizations, in contrast, tend to be defined by hierarchical relationships, structures, and controlling mechanisms. Communities are influenced more by values, purpose, professional relationships, collegiality, and the need for interdependence (p. 4). Organizations are characterized by approaches that tend to be impersonal, bureaucratic, and more concerned with preserving the status quo through external control. For Sergiovanni, the school perceived as an organization tends to be formal, distant, preoccupied with control issues, and highly technical. The school as community, however, is concerned with shared purpose, building relationships, and creating an atmosphere where people act out of deep personal concern for one another and their mutual welfare.

Sergiovanni (1994) places great emphasis on schools becoming purposeful communities, even above ones described as caring, learning, professional, collegial, inclusive, and inquiring (p. 71). Sergiovanni believes that a purposeful community is one where the members are bound together by a shared ideology and system norms that support those beliefs. Shared ideologies (shared vision, from our perspective) are what bind people together as a community and help them make sense out of their lives and work.

The notion of a professional community, for Sergiovanni, is heavily dependent on the concept of virtue. He believes that there is a general tendency to view professionalism from the perspective of a knowledge base required to inform practice. He also believes that there is a tendency for experts to conceive of their role as providing service to clients. The expert-client relationship is one that breeds impersonal relationships and dependency—values contrary to building community. Virtue comes from a commitment to share values that form the professional ideal for practice: a commitment to (a) practice in an exemplary way, (b) practice toward valued social ends, (c) not only to one's practice but to the practice itself, and (d) the ethic of caring (p. 142).

The professional ideal, if taken seriously, provides the normative foundation for the building of a professional community within a school. If teachers and administrators are committed to exemplary practice, they must remain current with the latest research and theory related to pedagogy. Not only is each individual committed to improving his or her own pedagogical techniques, the entire community of teachers is engaged in improving its performance. The concern for the total learning community means that teachers share pedagogical techniques in an open environment; they visit each other's classrooms and invite specialists to demonstrate new instructional techniques. In the words of Louis and Kruse (1995; see Chapter 6), teachers engage in the deprivatization of practice and take collective responsibility for student learning in the school.

The value of pursuing valued social ends is directed toward the concept of service. According to Sergiovanni (1994), the school community that places a premium on service to student, parents, and the broader community elevates the work of professionals to a level of stewardship—to a calling as opposed to an occupation (p. 145).

Learning communities are also inquiring communities. That is, members of the community continually reflect upon the culture of the school and the extent to which it is fulfilling its vision. The notion of inquiry means that all aspects of the school's operations must be open to scrutiny to verify that each aspect is serving the common good and the espoused vision. In the inquiring school, the goal is to become better than you currently are. Members of the community, the stakeholders, determine what they need to do to become a more effective learning community. They identify professional development needs and arrange for those needs to be fulfilled. They call in experts and specialists to help them achieve a higher level of performance. The emphasis here is on self-directed improvement strategies, not improvement strategies designed by someone outside the learning community.

An important characteristic of the school as a learning community is the ethic of caring. Schools must become caring communities where all stakeholders demonstrate a concern for the well-being of others, particularly students. It is at this level of caring that shared values become implemented and from these values that the moral authority of the school is established.

We have placed paramount importance on authentic learning throughout this book. Yet the importance of caring in the learning school should not be underestimated. As Fred Newmann has pointed out,

> There is more to life than academic achievement. Academic success must not, therefore, be the sole criterion for school membership. Students' moral worth and dignity must be affirmed through other avenues as well, such as nonacademic contact between staff and students. In short the separate features we identify (purpose, fairness, support, success) must be integrated within a more general climate of caring. (Newmann et al., 1992, p. 23)

In an extended analysis of what it means to care, Altenbaugh, Engel, and Martin (1995) state that what is fundamental to caring is apprehending the reality of another person (p. 159). They note that, by definition, caring involves feelings. As such, there is no single recipe or set of rules for caring. As these researchers put it, "What is required is willingness, concern, and empathy" (p. 160).

What we extract from this research and analysis is that a learning school is also a caring school. A caring environment reinforces learning. Establishing a caring environment dovetails with other elements of a professional community, such as the need to establish reasonable class size—for as class size is increased, a teacher's ability to reach all students in a caring manner is compromised.

Sergiovanni's emphasis on changing the metaphor for schools from organization to community recognizes the need for stakeholders to develop bonds of relationships that serve the common good. Learning communities acquire their moral authority through shared values. These shared values focus primarily on students' learning; however, the entire community must become one of learners. Teachers, administrators, parents, and community members all must continue to learn how they can serve each other in a caring community. All members must continue to learn how they can become better teachers, administrators, parents, and community members. They all must collectively inquire about improving the conditions of learning, work, governance, and caring. In short, the learning community must take the responsibility for continually improving its own well-being. As Sergiovanni (1994) states, "Building community in schools is about a shared quest to do things differently, to develop different kinds of relationships, to create new ties, to make new commitments" (p. 153).

The Learning Community and the Learning Organization

We believe that the concepts of Sergiovanni's learning community and Senge's learning organization are compatible. The two authors take different starting positions, however. Senge stresses the improvement of the organization through the effective application of the five disciplines of personal mastery, mental models, shared vision, team learning, and systems thinking. Senge's goal is to enable an organization to move from its current level of operation and become an effective learning organization. Sergiovanni, however, finds the metaphor of school as organization to be dysfunctional and proposes that we conceive of schools as communities.

We find Senge's concept of personal mastery and Sergiovanni's concept of the professional ideal to be similar when related to exemplary practice. Both concepts deal with individuals making a commitment to become the best possible worker or professional that they can become. For Senge, that means that people with a high level of personal mastery are engaged in continual learning for themselves and also for the organization. For Sergiovanni, the professional ideal requires people to improve their practice to an exemplary level not only for the individual but for the practice itself. Thus, in our view, personal mastery and the professional ideal embrace the same concept.

For Senge, mental models are the tacit assumptions, simple generalizations, or mental images and stories about how an organization works. Mental models shape the behavior of people and organizations; mental models typically are unverbalized "ways we do things around here." The power of mental models lies in the fact that they provide a frame of reference that determines how people perceive things. Two people witnessing the same event may perceive entirely different things because of the frame of reference they bring to the occasion. The power of mental models is that they can restrict vision or the ability of persons to see things differently. In a similar vein, Sergiovanni refers to the need to develop a new metaphor for schools because he finds the concept of schools as organizations to be dysfunctional. Sergiovanni's mental model of schools as organizations brings with it a frame of reference that views schools as bureaucratically controlled organizations that are insensitive to individuals and ineffective in serving the learning goals of the institution.

Sergiovanni proposes a shift to the mental model of school as community that provides a very different frame of reference. It is the norms of school as community that become the mental models; the norms of caring, inquiry, professionalism, and the like become the verbalized and unverbalized generalizations and assumptions that influence interpersonal relations and shape the school culture. The shift from the mental model of school as organization to school as community creates a very different mental image or vision. We believe that the concept of mental model and the norms of the school as a community refer to the same phenomena as they relate to the school as a learning community.

Senge's (1990) concept of shared vision and Sergiovanni's (1994) notion of shared values deal with the same phenomena, in our view. The concept of vision to Senge is that of a mental image of the future of the organization. Shared vision becomes the force that pulls an organization together—the common values that provide focus and goals for the learning organization. For Senge, shared vision is the sine qua non of the learning organization. Although shared visions have their origin in the visions of individuals, it is only when a group bonds to its shared values that an organization attains the vitality it needs to continually improve.

Sergiovanni does not use the concept of vision per se, but he writes extensively about the shared values that form the essence of community. It is these shared values that are the building blocks for the school as a community. These values place a premium on the development of positive personal relationships in a culture of caring; when implemented they help create the purposeful and professional community of learners that Sergiovanni espouses. The concepts of shared values and shared vision have the same meaning for us as authors of *The Learning School*.

Senge's concept of team learning and Sergiovanni's concept of the school as a learning community have much the same meaning. Team learning refers to the ability of the organization to fulfill its vision; it builds on personal mastery and shared vision to energize the members of the organization to accomplish their goals. It uses the medium of discussion and dialogue to achieve its purpose. Senge (1990) identifies insightful thinking, coordinated action, and team roles as three dimensions of team learning (pp. 236-237). Insightful thinking refers to the ability to think about complex issues and to use the mental resources of the team to achieve full analysis of a situation. Coordinated action refers to the ability of team members to build on each other's strengths and to be aware of each person's contribution to goal achievement. Each member also has a specific role to play in achieving completion of the organization's goals. Team members also play a key role in convincing other teams to achieve the organization's shared vision.

The concept of team learning is also central to Sergiovanni's (1994) learning community. Although he does not use the term specifically, he describes the need for members of the learning community to engage in inquiry, shared leadership, and authentic relationships (p. 155). Inquiry and learning transcend the boundaries of roles and hierarchies to create situations where everyone is a learner and everyone a teacher. In Sergiovanni's view, the reciprocal roles of teacher and learner that members of the learning community play create the conditions of team learning.

There is no direct counterpart in Sergiovanni's concept of the learning community that quite matches Senge's concept of systems thinking. Perhaps it is because Sergiovanni rejects the metaphor of school as organization. Sergiovanni, however, does deal with all aspects of the culture of the learning community as a complex whole. Senge's concept of systems thinking, on the other hand, emerges from the more technical view of causal loops, archetypes, and computer modeling from the business world. Causal loops refers to the need to view relationships among things not as linear but as a circle of causality that use reinforcing feedback loops. Archetypes refer to the structures that recur again and again in the behavior of people and organizations; they are the most common type of explanation of observed behavior. An example of an archetype in school change might be the passive resistance of individuals opposed to a change initiative. Computer modeling does not have a direct counterpart in thinking about the learning community in the learning school.

In summary, we believe that the concepts of the learning community proposed by Sergiovanni and the learning organization as described in the work of Senge and his colleagues have direct implications for our vision of the learning school.

The Professional Community as Viewed by Sergiovanni and Louis

The professional community proposed by Sergiovanni (1994) is characterized by what he describes as the professional ideal (see above). The professional ideal requires teachers and administrators to constantly improve their own professional expertise. Additionally, the professional ideal imposes a condition that teachers and administrators must engage each other in improving the overall quality of pedagogy or administration for the profession at large. Professional community fosters interdependence and collegiality.

Louis and Kruse (1995) have identified the five dimensions of a professional community as reflective dialogue, deprivatization of practice, focus on student learning, collaboration, and shared values (see Chapter 6). They also have identified the structural conditions that are necessary to support the creation of strong professional communities as (a) time to meet and talk, (b) physical proximity, (c) interdependent teaching roles, (d) communication structures and networks, and (e) teacher empowerment and school autonomy. Besides their own research, Louis and Kruse cite the work of Bryk and his colleagues at the University of Chicago who identified these additional human and social factors that support the professional community: openness to improvement, trust and respect, access to expertise, supportive leadership, and mechanisms to socialize new members (Bryk & Rollow, 1993, in Louis & Kruse, 1995). Building a professional community in schools is a complex task. Louis and Kruse believe, based on their analysis of data, that shared values and reflective dialogue are the most important factors that will likely promote the professional community.

We find the positions of Sergiovanni and Louis and Kruse on the professional community to be mutually reinforcing. Clearly, the commitment to practice and its improvement is present in both the professional ideal of Sergiovanni and the deprivatization of practice and reflective dialogue of Louis and Kruse. The concept of valued social ends (Sergiovanni) and shared values (Louis & Kruse) deal with the essence of a vision for a school. The notion of caring (Sergiovanni) and the collective responsibility for student learning (Louis & Kruse) embrace many of the same values.

Sergiovanni's position on the professional community comes from a theoretical perspective on the general concept of building community in schools, whereas Louis and Kruse's position emerges from research conducted in schools. Thus, they have a more comprehensive perspective than Sergiovanni has about the factors comprising the view of the professional community and the conditions needed to bring it about. Both perspectives are consistent with our vision of the learning school and are consistent, we believe, with our proposed integrated model (see Chapter 5).

The Integrated Model and the Professional Community

The integrated model and its components (vision, pedagogy, assessment, and governance) embrace both implicitly and explicitly the concept of the professional community, with governance structure our main locus. Governance is viewed very broadly in this context; it not only refers to the decision-making processes in which stakeholders engage but also to continuous professional growth of its members. Louis and Kruse (1995) found school autonomy and providing teachers with decision-making authority regarding instructional matters to be a facilitating condition for the development of the professional community.

In the integrated model, the concept of assessment is also broadly construed. Assessment of student learning consistent with the vision is of primary importance; however, gathering data to assess the climate of the school and to reflect on its operations is vital to the ongoing renewal of the school. The continuous renewal of the learning school requires the development of a professional community with all of the attributes described by Sergiovanni and by Louis and Kruse.

The learning school is one where all stakeholders engage in the continual reflection on practice to identify ways in which the operations of the school can be improved. The main focus is on improving student learning and providing the support conditions to facilitate that goal. A major part of that effort must be to establish the conditions where the professionals and other stakeholders can create the sense of community as a learning organization. Not only teachers and administrators but parents and community members must reflect on how they can contribute to the more effective operations of the school as a learning community. Parents and community members need to reflect on their roles in supporting the school and its main goal of improving student learning. In doing so, they model the essence of the learning community—the capacity to reflect on the current condition and the willingness to inquire about its improvement. Following reflection, the learning community accesses the specialized knowledge or expertise needed to move to higher levels of performance.

The learning school, the learning organization, and the learning community all embrace the same values. They imply the creation of norms, supporting mechanisms, and structural conditions that enable stakeholders to become problem seekers and problem solvers. The concept of problem seeker refers to both a continual search for better ways to improve the performance of the learning school and seeking conditions that need to be improved. The concept of problem solver refers to the ability of individuals and communities to engage in the process of creating and testing solutions to the problems identified. Taken together, problem seeking and problem solving identify two major processes that are necessary conditions for the learning community.

The Learning Community
in Case Studies

Two of the districts described in the case studies provide excellent examples of engaging the broader community in building and implementing the schools' vision (Beaver Area School District and Souhegan High School).

The Beaver Area School District describes itself as a learning organization in a learning community (see Chapter 8). As a learning organization, it embodies many of the key elements of Peter Senge's (1990) five disciplines previously described in this chapter. As a learning community, it exemplifies many of the elements of both community and professional community described by Sergiovanni (1994) and by Louis and Kruse (1995). The district's effort to reach out to the broader community to help it define the competencies of the graduate exemplifies the broadest connotations of the learning community. The definition of the graduate provided the driving force for the district's vision and stimulated the design of assessments, curricula, and instructional strategies used to achieve the vision. Beaver citizens worked with Superintendent Betty Sue Schaughency to define the attributes of the graduate and draft the strategic plan to achieve its implementation. The broad engagement of citizens in the Beaver Area School District provides one example of the learning community proposed by the authors.

Dr. Richard Lalley created another example of what we describe as a learning community. In designing Souhegan High School, Lalley engaged 125 citizens in an exploration of the values that the school should embody. Amherst citizens read and discussed books and materials from the Coalition of Essential Schools to help form their vision of the new high school. In this respect, the citizens acted as a learning community by engaging in reading, reflection, and discussion to reach consensus on the school's goals, policies, and practices. In the process, Lalley created deep meaning about the purpose of a high school education among the citizens. Engaging citizens in deliberations regarding the characteristics of the educational program, student policies, instructional practices, and the like created a significant learning community to support the launching of Souhegan High School.

The Three Levels of
the Learning Community

The learning community described in this chapter operates at three levels: student, professional, and community. At the first level, students are engaged by teachers and fellow students to pursue meaning making. They are involved in mastering the skills of learning how to learn and acquiring knowledge of the content of academic disciplines. The skills acquired and the knowledge gained help them engage in authentic learning (see Chapter 5) to pursue the goals of becoming active and effective problem seekers and problem solvers. The essence of the learning community for students is the pursuit of knowledge through active learning and meaning making.

For teachers and administrators in the schools, the second level of the learning community is exemplified in their professional community and in the learning organization. As a community, the professionals seek to improve their own pedagogical or leadership skills by engaging in study, reflection, dialogue, and the elicitation of feedback from each other. As a learning organization, they examine the policies, practices, and procedures that govern the operation of the school and they reflect on ways in which the operations of the schools could be more effective in serving the learning needs of students. Also, they examine ways in which the school's organization, practices, and policies serve to provide a highly effective and productive working environment for adults as they serve their primary clients—students and parents.

The third level of the learning community refers to the broad engagement of parents, community members, and community leaders in building and achieving the school's vision. The learning community needs to support the school in the pursuit of its vision. Parents, senior citizens, and community organizations and institutions all need to participate in the promotion of the goals of the learning community. Parents participate in the education of their children by supervising and assisting learning at home; they also support teachers and principals in their efforts to promote student learning. Senior citizens can provide their expertise through volunteering their talents and providing oral histories of the community. Community organizations and institutions, such as business or higher education institutions, can provide learning opportunities for students and help them perceive the relevance of school learning as to the world outside the school. Through the broad participation of community residents, businesses, and other institutions, the concept of the learning community reaches its broadest definition.

In the final analysis, the dynamic interaction between these levels of the learning community (student, professional, and other stakeholders) provides the basis for creating an institution that will continually re-create itself in the pursuit of more effective achievement of its vision that enlivens and sustains its growth.

Guidelines for Engaging
the Community

Throughout this book we have espoused the notion of engaging all stakeholders in identifying the core values and beliefs that form the basis of their vision. Three notable examples were provided in the case studies that exemplified community involvement: Schaughency in Beaver, Pennsylvania; Lalley in Amherst, New Hampshire; and Hampton in Fort Worth, Texas. Schaughency engaged over 300 members of the broader community in defining the graduate and in developing the strategic plan to implement that vision. Lalley engaged 125 community residents in a long-term study to identify the core values that would form the basis for reinventing high school education for the community; he engaged citizens in reading books and literature from the Coalition of Essential Schools. Hampton and her superintendent, Don Roberts, engaged business leaders from the Fort Worth area to identify the skills that graduates needed to be successfully employed in the economy of the region; they used these data to form the C^3 initiative and to craft an applied learning curriculum for elementary, middle, and high schools. These examples provide models that a principal or a superintendent could employ to engage the community in establishing a vision for his or her school or district.

In this section, we provide some guidelines culled from the case studies that will help schools and districts think about ways in which they can involve the community's stakeholders. Engaging the broader community in the learning school is important to build the covenant of shared values that will govern the learning community. Community engagement is necessary to achieve the financial and moral support that the schools need to fulfill their vision and their mission. We offer the following guidelines for engaging the learning community:

1. Provide stakeholders with the opportunity to explore their values and beliefs through presentations, data gathering, or

readings that provide the substance for discussions ultimately leading to their statement of the vision for the school or district.

2. Engage stakeholders in extended discussions to elicit the learning outcomes they wish students to demonstrate when they graduate from the school or district.

3. Lead stakeholders to identify the core values and beliefs that undergird their vision of the graduate.

4. Lead the stakeholders to identify the data that will be acceptable to verify that a graduate has attained the learning outcomes specified in the vision; and provide the school or district professionals with technical support to identify or develop assessment measures that will gather information to validate attainment of learning outcomes.

5. Create periodic forums where all stakeholders can meet to evaluate the progress of the school in attaining its vision; and provide opportunities to affirm or modify the vision statement based on experience.

6. Develop a variety of communication devices to report progress of the school or district as it works toward vision attainment.

7. Provide appropriate training for stakeholders to improve the quality of discourse, to engage in shared decision making and to pursue effective problem solving and conflict resolution.

8. Create opportunities for students, professionals, parents, and community members to celebrate the accomplishments of students, the school, and the district in the progressive attainment of its vision.

Summary

In this chapter, we described the essential elements of the learning community as it evolves from the learning school and proposed that the learning community operates at three levels—the student level, the professional level, and the community level.

We reviewed the salient features of Senge's learning organization and provided examples of how each of his five disciplines applies to the learning school. We then summarized the key features of the school as a learning community as defined by Sergiovanni. We used his proposal that the metaphor of the school be changed from the school as organization to the school as community. We then compared the elements of Senge's learning organization with Sergiovanni's concepts of the learning community.

We compared the concept of a professional community as presented by Sergiovanni with that provided by Louis and Kruse. Those conceptions were found to be similar to the role of the professional community in our integrated model.

Finally, we provided a set of guidelines that schools or districts can use to engage the broader community as full members of the learning community.

Epilogue

Developing a learning school in practice is not a simple or easy task, but it can be an exciting one. We suggest that our experience is more interesting and satisfying when the day begins with challenges and a sense of direction (vision) for dealing with them.

For each reader of this book, the challenge of a new day is ever present. Why not respond by making yours a learning school?

Appendix A

Three Rivers School District
Analysis of Probability Statements

The Three Rivers School District needs to consider three major forces—economic, social, and political—that will have an impact on the future of education in the district.

The priority when analyzing these major forces in education is to consider the significant differences present within the given category. Each force has many variables that may have a greater probability of impact upon the district. Listed on page 187 are the major forces within the Three Rivers School District and the respective probability (in terms of percentage) of most critical developments for the district.

The analysis of these probability statements demonstrates the underlying messages throughout the district. These issues will impact vision choice for several years to come. It is clear that issues in Three Rivers will revolve around finances. The highest probability in economic issues relates to taxes and a demand for fiscal accountability. The political forces also relate to money in terms of unfunded mandates and special interest group activity. Special interest can translate into dollars when programs are being sought. The last area, social forces, has the highest probability in the single-parent category, which can also translate into single income.

The analysis of probability statements clearly demonstrates the formative beginning of a vision statement.

AUTHORS' NOTE: The materials included in Appendixes A, B, and C were prepared by the following students in the Superintendents Academy, University of Pittsburgh: Michael Bjalobok, Edward Drugo, Mary Ann Fusco, Kevin McGuire, and Carol Polkinghorn.

Three Rivers School District Analysis of Probability Statements

---

Economic

More concern and sensitivity to tax increases	90
More wage concessions being sought	60
More citizens demanding fiscal accountability	90
More unfunded state and federal mandates or cutbacks	80
Districts need to become capital intensive and computerize	85

Social

Increasing elderly population	70
Increased single-parent or single-income or latchkey kids	85
Increased negativity in media and rise of values	70
Increased fragmentation and home schooling	80
Reaffirmation of existing social structures and classes	75

Political

More unfunded mandates	80
Increased block granting	75
Increased special interest group activity	90
Lower voter turnout	80
Voucher, charters, and privatization on horizon	85

Appendix B

Three Rivers School District:
Scenario—Authenticity, 2010

As the year 2010 begins, economic constraints have dramatically impacted life in America. The country's struggle to remain competitive in the global marketplace has resulted in a loss of new job opportunities. To become more competitive, local employers are demanding that high school students graduate with entry-level job skills and that all students be effective decision makers, problem solvers, and communicators. Economic constraints have also increased the demand for fiscal accountability in all institutions. In addition, the information superhighway now provides limitless possibilities for networking within the global marketplace.

Socially, children continue to be at risk due to the large percentage of single-parent and dysfunctional families. Decreased government funding of family support programs has limited the population of 1940s' baby boomers and has financially strained government support systems. To supplement the needs of the elderly, all able-bodied youths must be part of a productive, competitive, and skilled workforce. Special interest groups continue to impact government funding of public education by creating charter and private schools.

Trends in education are consistent with the above. Public demand for accountability has resulted in a constituency-driven education system from which taxpayers demand measurable results. Students must demonstrate what they know and can do as a result of their tax-funded education. Through the work of its school-community management team, Three Rivers School District has developed a list of competencies and a menu of authentic learning experiences for all graduates. Successful adults across the community volunteer to demonstrate and model authentic work for students.

Parents and other adults team with school personnel to evaluate student performance of competencies and high intellectual standards. Local business and industry personnel provide resources for authentic instruction and assessment tasks. The local community is responding positively to its open involvement in educational planning, implementation, and evaluation.

Active involvement of community members and parents in the schools provides a larger mentor population for students lacking an extended family or demonstrating special needs. The goal of mentors is to encourage success for all students. Authentic pedagogy has also created equal opportunities for students regardless of gender, race, ethnicity, or socioeconomic status. Students are socially enriched by a curriculum that encourages risk taking and independent thinking and by a climate that fosters mutual respect for all members.

In a time when all students must become productive members of the workforce, authenticity is highly motivating to students. They practice sustaining the hard work that learning requires by addressing real-world problems. As a result, students have a stake in their work and value learning. Overall, the mastery gained in school transfers to life beyond school and increases the efficiency of the public investment in schooling.

Students in the Three Rivers School District cultivate higher-order thinking skills and problem-solving abilities to increase their global competitiveness. The information superhighway has opened the world of Three Rivers School District. Neighboring school districts, colleges, and the local businesses and industries have pooled their resources with Three Rivers to network the latest in technology for the students and the community. Authentic pedagogy requires accessing these tools and resources.

With a dramatic turnover in faculty during the past 10 years, Three Rivers School District has made a significant financial commitment to staff development opportunities for both new and experienced staff members. This collaborative effort with local businesses and industries has resulted in shared training resources. Teachers also are experiencing authentic learning opportunities through teacher residencies. These real-world programs enhance their understanding of the skills and concepts necessary for all students to achieve success in the 21st century. These experiences have also enhanced communication and fostered respect between all parties in this constituency-driven system focused on authentic pedagogy.

Appendix C

Table 1 How Good Are the Vision Statements?

	Alternatives			
Criteria	*1*	*2*	*3*	*4*
Future oriented?	5	5	1	5
Utopian?	5	5	1	4
Appropriate?	3	1	4	2
Reflects high ideals?	5	3	1	5
Clarifies purpose?	4	2	5	5
Inspires enthusiasm?	3	3	2	3
Reflects uniqueness?	3	2	3	4
Ambitious?	5	5	1	5

NOTE: Alternatives rated from 1 (low) to 5 (high).

TABLE 2 Vision Statement With Weighted Criteria

		Alternatives			
Criteria	*Relative Weight*	*1*	*2*	*3*	*4*
Future oriented?	10	50	50	10	50
Utopian?	10	50	50	10	40
Appropriate?	7	21	7	28	14
Reflects high ideals?	9	45	27	9	45
Clarifies purpose?	9	36	18	45	45
Inspires enthusiasm?	8	24	24	16	24
Reflects uniqueness?	6	18	12	18	24
Ambitious?	5	25	25	5	25
	Total	269	213	141	267

NOTE: Criteria assigned relative weights from 1 (low) to 10 (high).

TABLE 3 Comparing Vision Alternatives With Measures of Success

	Vision Alternatives			
Measures of Success	*1*	*2*	*3*	*4*
Enhanced student achievement	5	3	4	5
Increased school completion rate	5	3	4	5
Enhanced faculty and student morale	4	2	2	4
Effective student programs	4	4	2	4
Effective faculty development	4	3	2	3
Effective organizational development	3	4	3	4
Postsecondary continuation	5	3	4	4
Safe and supportive schools	2	2	4	3
Public engagement	5	2	2	3

NOTE: Success criteria rated alternatives from 1 (low) to 5 (high).

TABLE 4 Weighted Comparison of Vision Alternatives With Measures of Success

		Vision Alternatives			
Measures of Success	*Relative Weight*	*1*	*2*	*3*	*4*
Enhanced student achievement	10	50	30	40	50
Increased school completion rate	10	50	30	40	50
Enhanced faculty and student morale	7	28	14	14	28
Effective student programs	5	20	20	10	20
Effective faculty development	6	24	18	12	18
Effective organizational development	7	21	28	21	28
Postsecondary continuation	8	40	24	32	32
Safe and supportive schools	7	14	14	28	21
Public engagement	9	45	18	18	27
	Total	292	196	215	274

NOTE: Success criteria assigned relative weights from 1 (low) to 10 (high).

TABLE 5 Comparing Vision Alternatives on Organizational Synergy

	Vision Alternatives			
Consistency With:	*1*	*2*	*3*	*4*
District's cultures and values	3	2	2	3
District's strengths	2	3	3	2
Stakeholders' needs				
Students	5	2	3	3
Faculty	4	2	3	3
Administrators	3	2	2	2
Parents	2	2	2	2
Community leaders	1	1	1	1
Technology	4	5	4	4

NOTE: Success criteria rated alternatives from 1 (low) to 5 (high).

TABLE 6 Weighted Comparison of Vision Alternatives on Organizational Synergy

		Vision Alternatives			
Consistency With:	*Relative Weight*	*1*	*2*	*3*	*4*
District's cultures and values	9	27	18	18	27
District's strengths	9	18	27	27	18
Stakeholders' needs					
Students	10	50	20	30	30
Faculty	7	28	14	14	21
Administrators	5	15	10	10	10
Parents	6	12	12	18	12
Community leaders	5	5	5	10	5
Technology	7	28	35	21	28
	Total	183	141	148	151

NOTE: Assessing relative weights for organizational synergy from 1 (low) to 10 (high).

TABLE 7 Summing the Evaluation of Alternatives

Totals From:		*Aternatives*			
		1	2	3	4
Table 2		269	213	141	267
Table 4		292	196	215	274
Table 6		183	141	148	151
	Total	744	550	504	692

References

Altenbaugh, R. J., Engel, D. E., & Martin, D. T. (1995). *Caring for kids: A critical study of urban school leavers.* London: Falmer.

Ausubel, D. P. (1963). *The psychology of meaningful verbal learning.* New York: Green & Stratton.

Barker, J. A. (1989). *Discovering the future: The business of paradigms* [Videotape]. Burnsville, NM: Chart House Learning Corporation.

Barker, J. A. (1990). *Discovering the future: The power of vision* [Videotape]. Burnsville, NM: Chart House Learning Corporation.

Barth, R. (1990). *Improving schools from within.* San Francisco: Jossey Bass.

Beaver Area commences strategic planning process. (1993a). *Beaver Area School District Newsletter, 15*(2), 4-5. (Available from Beaver Area School District, 855 Second Street, Beaver, PA 15009)

Beaver Area School District defines its graduate of the future. (1993b). *Beaver Area School District Newsletter, 16*(1), 1. (Available from Beaver Area School District, 855 Second Street, Beaver, PA 15009)

Beaver Area School District Strategic Plan. (1993). (Available from Beaver Area School District, 855 Second Street, Beaver, PA 15009)

Beaver Area School District: A learning organization reaching into a learning community. (1995). [Brochure]. (Available from Beaver Area School District, 855 Second Street, Beaver, PA 15009)

Beck, I. L., & Carpenter, P. A. (1986). Cognitive approaches to understanding reading. *American Psychologist, 41*(10), 1098-1105.

Bennett, K. P., & LeCompte, M. D. (1990). *The way schools work: A sociological analysis of education.* New York: Longman.

Bennis, W., & Nanus, B. (1985). *Leaders: The strategies for taking charge.* New York: HarperCollins.

Berger, P. L., & Luckmann, T. (1966). *The social construction of reality.* New York: Doubleday.

Boyer, E. L. (1983). *High School: A report on secondary education in America.* New York: Harper & Row.

Brooks & Brooks (1993). *The case for constructivist classrooms.* Alexandria, VA: Association for Supervision and Curriculum Development.

Bruer, J. T. (1993). *Schools for thought.* Cambridge, MA: MIT Press.

Bruner, J. S. (1960). *The process of education.* Cambridge, MA: Harvard University Press.

Bruner, J. S. (1961). Act of discovery. *Harvard Educational Review, 31,* 21-23.

Chipman, S. F. (1992). The higher order cognitive skills: What they are and how they might be transmitted. In T. G. Sticht, B. S. McDonald, & M. J. Beeler (Eds.), *The intergenerational transfer of cognitive skills.* Norwood, NJ: Ablex.

Cole, H. P. (1973). *Process oriented education: The new direction for elementary-secondary schools.* Englewood, NJ: Educational Technology.

Comer, J. P. (1980). *School power.* New York: Free Press.

Covey, S. R. (1989). *The seven habits of highly effective people.* New York: Fireside, Simon & Schuster.

Csikszentmihalyi, M. (1990). Literacy and intrinsic motivation. *Daedalus, 119*(2), 118.

Cuban, L. (1984). *How teachers taught: Change and constancy in American classrooms, 1890-1980.* New York: Longman.

Deming, W. E. (1986). *Out of the crisis.* Cambridge: MIT-CAES.

Deming, W. E. (1987). The Deming library, Volume II [Videotape]. Chicago: Films Incorporated.

Dewey, J. (1916). *Democracy and education.* New York: Macmillan.

Dewey, J. (1929). *Experience and nature.* LaSalle, IL: Opencourt Publishing.

Dewey, J. (1963). *Experience and education.* New York: Collier.

Dewey, J., & Bentley, A. F. (1949). *Knowing and the known.* Boston: Beacon.

Dobyns, L., & Crawford-Mason, C. (1991). *Quality or else: The revolution in world business.* Boston: Houghton Mifflin.

Eisner, E. (1991). *The enlightened eye: Qualitative inquiry and the enhancement of educational practice.* New York: Macmillan.

Farnham-Diggory, S. (1990). *Schooling.* Cambridge, MA: Harvard University Press.

Gagne, R. M., & Brown, L. T. (1961). Some factors in the programming of conceptual learning. *Journal of Experimental Psychology, 62,* 313-321.

Gagne, R. M., & Smith, E. C., Jr. (1965). A study of the effects of verbalization on problem solving. In R. C. Anderson & D. P. Ausubel

(Eds.), *Readings in the psychology of cognition* (pp. 380-391). New York: Holt, Reinhart & Winston.

Gardner, H. (1988). *Frames of mind: The theory of multiple intelligences.* New York: Basic Books.

Gardner, H. (1991). *The unschooled mind.* New York: Basic Books.

Glasser, W. (1984). *Control theory.* New York: Harper & Row.

Glasser, W. (1990). *The quality school.* New York: Harper & Row.

Goodlad, J. I. (1984). *A place called school.* New York: McGraw-Hill.

Graham, P. (Ed.). (1995). *Mary Parker Follett: Prophet of management.* Boston: Harvard Business School Press.

Green, T. F. (1971). *The activities of teaching.* New York: McGraw-Hill.

Hackman, J. R., & Oldham, G. (1976). Motivation through the design of work: A test of theory. *Organizational Management Review, 16*(2), 250-279.

Heifetz, R. A. (1994). *Leadership without easy answers.* Cambridge, MA: Belknap.

Husserl, E. (1964). *The idea of phenomenology* (W. P. Alston & G. Nakhnikian, Trans.). The Hague, The Netherlands: Martinus Nihoff.

Johnson, S. M. (1996). *Lead to change: The challenge of the new superintendency.* San Francisco: Jossey-Bass.

Kerchner, C. T., & Koppich, J. E. (1993). *A union of professionals: Labor relations and educational reform.* New York: Teachers College Press.

Kittell, J. E. (1957). An experimental study of the effect of external direction during learning on transfer and retention of principles. *Journal of Educational Psychology, 48,* 391-405.

Kneller, G. F. (1984). *Movements of thought in modern education.* New York: John Wiley.

Louis, K. S., & Kruse, S. D. (1995). *Professionalism and community: Perspectives on reforming urban schools.* Thousand Oaks, CA: Corwin.

Louis, K. S., Marks, H. M., & Kruse, S. D. (1994). *Teachers' professional community in restructuring schools.* Madison: Wisconsin Center for Educational Research.

McBride, M. E. (1991). *A proposal to restructure McCleary elementary school.* Pittsburgh, PA: Pittsburgh Public Schools.

Merriam Webster's collegiate dictionary (10th ed.). (1993). Springfield, MA: Merriam Webster.

Mooney, J. E. (1990). *Ideology in school governance.* Unpublished doctoral dissertation, University of Pittsburgh.

Nanus, B. (1992). *Visionary leadership.* San Francisco: Jossey-Bass.

Newell, A., & Simon, H. A. (1972). *Human problem solving.* Englewood Cliffs, NJ: Prentice Hall.

Newmann, F. M. (1991). Linking restructuring to authentic student achievement. *Phi Delta Kappan, 72*(6), 458-463.

Newmann, F. M., Secada, W. G., & Wehlage, G. G. (1995). *A guide to authentic instruction and assessment: Vision, standards and scoring.* Madison: Wisconsin Center for Educational Research.

Newmann, F. M., & Wehlage, G. G. (1993). Five standards of authentic instruction. *Educational Leadership, 50*(7), 8-12.

Newmann, F. M., & Wehlage, G. G. (1995). *Successful school restructuring.* Madison, WI: Center on Organization and Restructuring Schools.

Newmann, F. M., Wehlage, G. G., & Lamborn, S. D. (1992). The significance and sources of student engagement. In F. M. Newmann (Ed.), *Student engagement and achievement in American secondary schools.* New York: Teachers College Press

Newmann, F. M., & Associates (1996). *Authentic achievement: Restructuring schools for intellectual quality.* San Francisco: Jossey-Bass.

Niebuhr, R. (1935). *An interpretation of christian ethics.* New York: Scribner's.

Noddings, N. (1984). *Caring: A feminist approach to ethics and moral education.* Berkeley: University of California.

O'Neil, J. (1995). On schools as learning organizations: A conversation with Peter Senge. *Educational Leadership, 52,* 20-23.

Phenix, P. H. (1964). *Realms of meaning: A philosophy of the curriculum for general education.* New York: McGraw-Hill.

Phillips, D. C., & Soltis, J. F. (1985). *Perspectives in learning.* New York: Teachers College Press.

Pittman, R. B., & Haughwout, P. (1987). Influence of high school size on dropout rate. *Educational Evaluation and Policy Analysis, 9,* 337-343.

Pittsburgh strategic implementation plan for restructuring. (1995). (Available from Pittsburgh Public Schools, 341 South Bellefield Avenue, Pittsburgh, PA 15213)

Powell, A. G., Farrar, E., & Cohen, D. K. (1985). *The shopping mall high school: Winners and losers in the educational marketplace.* Boston: Houghton Mifflin.

Resnick, L. B. (1986). *Education and learning to think: A special report prepared for the commission on behavioral and social sciences education.* Washington DC: National Research Council.

Resnick, L. B. (1995). *From the bell curve to all children can learn* [adapted from a video lecture]. Pittsburgh, PA: University of Pittsburgh, Institute for Learning, Learning Research and Development Center.

Rothman, R. (1996). *Organizing so all children can learn: Applying the principles of learning*. Pittsburgh, PA: University of Pittsburgh, Institute for Learning, Learning Research and Development Center.

Scardamalia, M., & Bereiter, C. (1987). Knowledge telling and knowledge transforming in written composition. In S. Rosenberg (Ed.), *Advances in applied psycholinguistics* (Vol. 2). Cambridge, UK: Cambridge University Press.

Scheffler, I. (1966). *The language of education*. Springfield, IL.: Charles C. Thomas.

Senge, P. M. (1990). *The fifth discipline: The art and practice of the learning organization*. New York: Doubleday.

Senge, P. M., Kleiner, A., Roberts, C., Ross, R. B., & Smith, B. J. (1994). *The fifth discipline fieldbook: Strategies and tools for building a learning organization*. New York: Doubleday.

Sergiovanni, T. J. (1992). *Moral leadership: Getting to the heart of school improvement*. San Francisco: Jossey-Bass.

Sergiovanni, T. J. (1994). *Building community in schools*. San Francisco: Jossey-Bass.

Sizer, T. R. (1984). *Horace's compromise*. Boston: Houghton Mifflin.

Stiggins, R. J. (1994). *Student-centered classroom assessment*. New York: Macmillan.

Suchman, J. R. (1962). *The elementary school training program in scientific enquiry*. Urbana: University of Illinois, Illinois College of Education.

Wisdom, J. (1957). *Philosophy and psychoanalysis*. Oxford, UK: Basil Blackwell.

Yukl, G. A. (1989). *Leadership in Organizations* (2nd ed.). Englewood Cliffs, NJ: Prentice Hall.

Index